INTERACTIVE
COMPUTING
SOFTWARE SKILLS

Microsoft®
Word 97

Kenneth C. Laudon
Azimuth Multimedia Productions, Inc

Michael Banino

Irwin
McGraw-Hill

Boston   Burr Ridge, IL   Dubuque, IA   Madison, WI   New York   San Francisco   St. Louis
Bangkok   Bogotá   Caracas   Lisbon   London   Madrid
Mexico City   Milan   New Delhi   Seoul   Singapore   Sydney   Taipei   Toronto

Irwin/McGraw-Hill

A Division of The **McGraw·Hill** Companies

Interactive Computing Software Skills
Microsoft® Word 97

3 4 5 6 7 8 9 0 CRS 7 6 5 4 3 2 1 0 9

ISBN 0-07-038437-1

Editorial director: *Michael Junior*
Sponsoring editor: *Rhonda Sands*
Marketing manager: *James Rogers*
Project manager: *Richard DeVitto*
Cover designer: *Amanda Kavanagh*
Interior design: *Yvonne Quirk*
Development: *Jane Laudon*
Layout: *Evan Kantor, Michael Banino*
Compositor: *Pat Rogondino*
Printer: *Courier Stoughton*

Library of Congress Cataloging-in-Publication Data

Laudon, Kenneth C., 1944-
    Interactive computing software skills : Microsoft Word for Windows 95 /
Kenneth C. Laudon, Michael Banino.
        p.   cm.
        Includes index.
        ISBN 0-07-038437-1
    1. Microsoft Word for Windows) 2. Word Processing I. Banino,
Michael. II. Title.
    Z52.5.M523L38 1997
    652.5'5369--dc21   97-2210
                                                            CIP

http://www.mhhe.com

Contents

Contents (continued)

Preface

Interactive Computing:
Software Skills
Microsoft Office 97

· ·

The *Interactive Computing: Software Skills* series provides you with an illustrated interactive environment for learning introductory software skills using Microsoft Office 97. The Interactive Computing Series is composed of both illustrated books and multimedia interactive CD-ROMs for Windows 95 and each Office 97 program: Word 97, Excel 97, Access 97, and PowerPoint 97.

The books and the CD-ROMs are closely coordinated. The coverage of basic skills is the same in CDs and books, although the books go into more advanced skill areas. Because of their close coordination, the books and CD-ROMs can be used together very effectively, or they can each be used as stand-alone learning tools. The multimedia interactive CD-ROMs get you started very quickly on basic and intermediate skills. The books cover this material and then go farther.

It's up to you. You can choose how you want to learn. In either case the Interactive Computing Series gives you the easiest and most powerful way to learn Microsoft Office 97.

Skills, Concepts, and Steps

In both the book and the CD-ROM, each lesson is organized around *skills*, *concepts*, and *steps*. Each lesson is divided into a number of skills. The basic concept of each skill is first explained, including where that skill is used in practical work situations. The concept is then followed by a series of concise instructions or steps that the student follows to learn the skill. A *running case study* throughout reinforces the skill by giving a real-world focus to the learning process.

The Learning Approach

We have taken a highly graphical and multimedia approach to learning. Text, screen shots, graphics, and on the CD-ROM, voice, video, and digital world simulation are all used to teach concepts and skills. The result is a powerful learning package.

Using the Book

In the book, each skill is described in a two-page graphical spread (Figure 1). The left side of the two-page spread describes the skill, the concept, and the steps needed to perform the skill. The right side of the spread uses screen shots to show you how the screen should look at key stages.

Figure 1

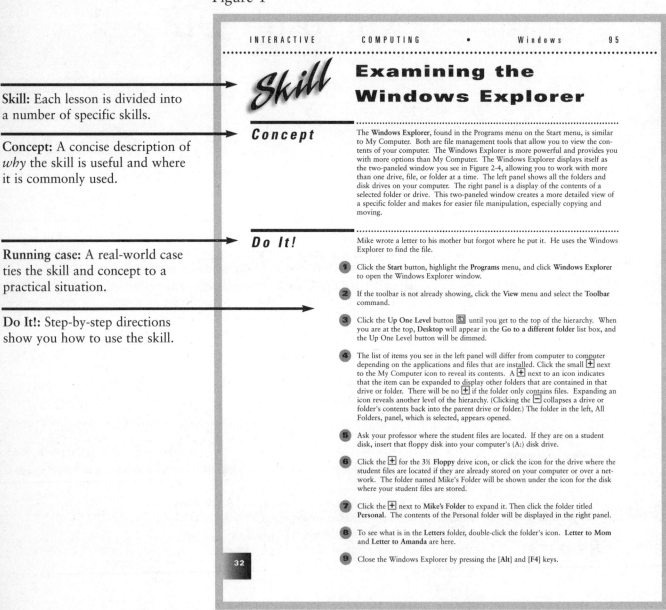

Skill: Each lesson is divided into a number of specific skills.

Concept: A concise description of *why* the skill is useful and where it is commonly used.

Running case: A real-world case ties the skill and concept to a practical situation.

Do It!: Step-by-step directions show you how to use the skill.

Inside the figure:

Skill

Examining the Windows Explorer

Concept

The **Windows Explorer**, found in the Programs menu on the Start menu, is similar to My Computer. Both are file management tools that allow you to view the contents of your computer. The Windows Explorer is more powerful and provides you with more options than My Computer. The Windows Explorer displays itself as the two-paneled window you see in Figure 2-4, allowing you to work with more than one drive, file, or folder at a time. The left panel shows all the folders and disk drives on your computer. The right panel is a display of the contents of a selected folder or drive. This two-paneled window creates a more detailed view of a specific folder and makes for easier file manipulation, especially copying and moving.

Do It!

Mike wrote a letter to his mother but forgot where he put it. He uses the Windows Explorer to find the file.

1. Click the **Start** button, highlight the **Programs** menu, and click **Windows Explorer** to open the Windows Explorer window.

2. If the toolbar is not already showing, click the **View** menu and select the **Toolbar** command.

3. Click the **Up One Level** button 🗐 until you get to the top of the hierarchy. When you are at the top, **Desktop** will appear in the **Go to a different folder** list box, and the Up One Level button will be dimmed.

4. The list of items you see in the left panel will differ from computer to computer depending on the applications and files that are installed. Click the small ⊞ next to the My Computer icon to reveal its contents. A ⊞ next to an icon indicates that the item can be expanded to display other folders that are contained in that drive or folder. There will be no ⊞ if the folder only contains files. Expanding an icon reveals another level of the hierarchy. (Clicking the ⊟ collapses a drive or folder's contents back into the parent drive or folder.) The folder in the left, All Folders, panel, which is selected, appears opened.

5. Ask your professor where the student files are located. If they are on a student disk, insert that floppy disk into your computer's (A:) disk drive.

6. Click the ⊞ for the 3½ **Floppy** drive icon, or click the icon for the drive where the student files are located if they are already stored on your computer or over a network. The folder named Mike's Folder will be shown under the icon for the disk where your student files are stored.

7. Click the ⊞ next to **Mike's Folder** to expand it. Then click the folder titled **Personal**. The contents of the Personal folder will be displayed in the right panel.

8. To see what is in the **Letters** folder, double-click the folder's icon. **Letter to Mom** and **Letter to Amanda** are here.

9. Close the Windows Explorer by pressing the [**Alt**] and [**F4**] keys.

32

End-of-Lesson Features

In the book, the learning in each lesson is reinforced at the end by a quiz and a skills review called Interactivity, which provides a step-by-step exercise and a real-world problem to solve independently.

Figure 1 (continued)

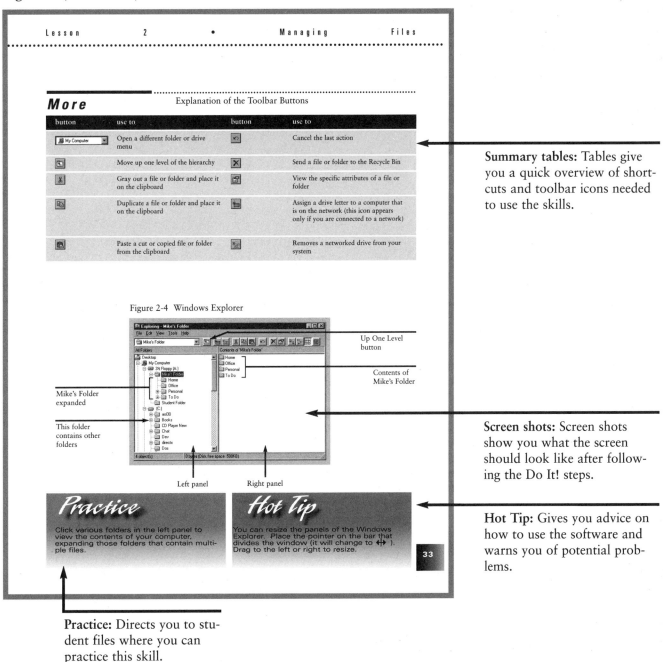

Summary tables: Tables give you a quick overview of short-cuts and toolbar icons needed to use the skills.

Screen shots: Screen shots show you what the screen should look like after following the Do It! steps.

Hot Tip: Gives you advice on how to use the software and warns you of potential problems.

Practice: Directs you to student files where you can practice this skill.

Using the Interactive CD-ROM

The Interactive Computing multimedia CD-ROM provides an unparalleled learning environment in which you can learn software skills faster and better than in books alone. The CD-ROM provides a unique interactive environment in which you can learn to use software faster and remember it better. The CD-ROM uses the same lessons, skills, concepts, and Do It! steps as found in the book, but presents the material using voice, video, animation, and precise simulation of the software you are learning. A typical CD-ROM contents screen shows the major elements of a lesson (Figure 2).

Figure 2

Skills list: A list of skills permits you to jump directly to any skill you want to learn or review.

Lessons and skills: The lessons and skills covered in the CD are closely coordinated with those of the book.

Interactive sessions: The skills you learn are immediately tested in interactive sessions with the TeacherWizard.

Review: At the end of each lesson is a review of all the concepts covered, as well as review questions.

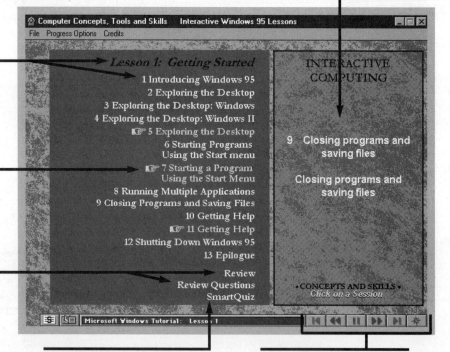

SmartQuiz: Each lesson has a SmartQuiz that tests your ability to accomplish tasks within a simulated software environment.

User controls: Precise and simple user controls permit you to start, stop, pause, jump forward or backward a sentence, or jump forward or backward an entire skill. A single Navigation Star takes you back to the lesson's table of contents.

Unique Features of the CD-ROM: TeacherWizards™ and SmartQuiz™

Interactive Computing: Software Skills offers many leading-edge features of the CD-ROM currently found in no other learning product on the market. One such feature is *interactive exercises* in which you are asked to demonstrate your command of a software skill in a precisely simulated software environment. Your actions are closely followed by a digital TeacherWizard that guides you with additional information if you make a mistake. When you correctly complete the action called for by the TeacherWizard, you are congratulated and prompted to continue the lesson. If you make a mistake, the TeacherWizard gently lets you know: "No, that's not the right icon. Click on the Open File icon at the left side of the toolbar on top of the screen." No matter how many mistakes you make, the TeacherWizard is there to help you.

Another leading-edge feature is the end-of-lesson SmartQuiz. Unlike the multiple choice and matching questions found in the book quiz, the SmartQuiz puts you in a simulated digital software world and asks you to show your mastery of skills while actually working with the software (Figure 3).

Figure 3

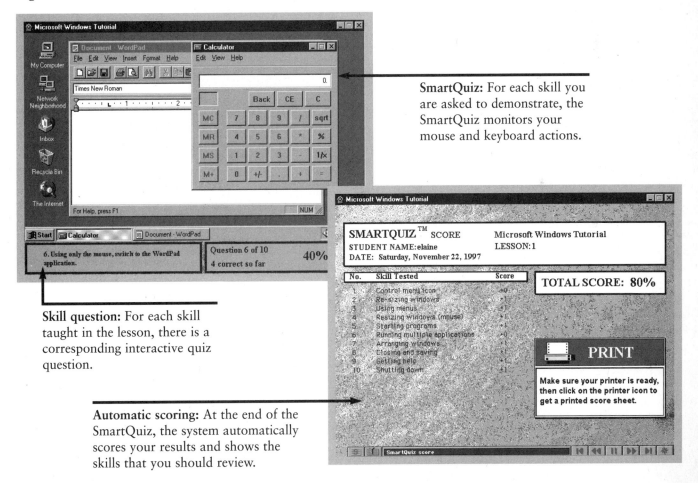

SmartQuiz: For each skill you are asked to demonstrate, the SmartQuiz monitors your mouse and keyboard actions.

Skill question: For each skill taught in the lesson, there is a corresponding interactive quiz question.

Automatic scoring: At the end of the SmartQuiz, the system automatically scores your results and shows the skills that you should review.

Using the CD-ROM and the Book Together

The CD-ROM and the book are designed to support each another. There is a close correspondence between the lessons and skills taught in the book and the CD for introductory levels of the software (Lessons 1 through 4), as well as between the case study used in the CDs and the books. Generally, the books have more lessons and go farther into advanced topics than the CD does, while the CD-ROM demonstrates the basic steps in more detail. Here are tips on using the CD and accompanying book together:

- You can use the book and the CD together at your student lab workstation or at home. Place them side by side and follow along in both at the same time.

- You can use the book when you do not have access to a computer, and use the CD by itself at school or at home.

- You can use the CD first to gain a quick understanding of the software, then use the book later at home or school ro review and deepen your understanding.

Student Files

The *Interactive Computing: Software Skills* books require that students have access to accompanying student files for the practice and test sessions. The instructor and students using the texts in class are granted the right to post the student files on any network or stand-alone computer, or to distribute the files on individual diskettes. You can download the student files from the Interactive Computing Web site at **http://www.mhhe.com/cit/apps/laudon/**, or request them through your Irwin/McGraw-Hill representative.

Supplementary Learning and Teaching Tools

The Student Center at http://www.mhhe.com/cit/apps/laudon/ provides the following supporting information:

- Web exercises: These exercises can be assigned by your instructor. Or you can try them on your own. Your instructor has the solutions.

- Cool sites: Web news, new technology, Web opportunities, entertainment.

- Message board: Talk to other students who are using the series.

- Multimedia action: Cool demos.

- Course help: Choose the course you're enrolled in. Then choose exercises, multimedia demos, free software, or course information.

The Faculty Lounge at http://www.mhhe.com/cit/apps/laudon/ provides the following instructional support:

- Exercises and solutions

- Teaching strategies

- Instructor message board

- Multimedia action

- Cool Web site

- Course help

Local Area Network Testing Facility

McGraw-Hill and Azimuth Multimedia have designed and produced a revolutionary and unique Network Testing Facility™ (NTF) that tests acquired software skills in a safe, simulated software environment. Operating on a network, the NTF permits students to take a self-paced exam from their workstations at home, at school, or in the classroom. The NTF automatically tracks student scores, and allows the instructor to build screens that indicate an individual student's progress or which skills may need more emphasis for the entire class.

Contact your McGraw-Hill representative for further information on the NTF.

Acknowledgments

The Interactive Computing Series is a cooperative effort of many individuals, each contributing to a team effort. Our goal is to provide students and instructors with the most powerful and enjoyable learning environment using both traditional text and new multimedia techniques. Achieving this goal requires the contributions of text authors, multimedia screenplay writers, multimedia designers, animators, graphic artists, editors, computer scientists, and student testers.

Our special thanks to Frank Ruggirello, who envisioned and initiated the Interactive Computing Series. Peter Jovanovich and Gary Burke of McGraw-Hill management generously supported a technological leap into the future of teaching and learning. Rhonda Sands, our editor, has gently pushed us to higher levels of performance and encouraged us to do the best we can.

Skills

L E S S O N

1

Introduction to Word

Microsoft® Word 97 is a word processing software program designed to make the creation of professional-quality documents fast and easy. Word allows the user to edit, move, and copy what has been written, providing enormous flexibility in how the finished product will appear.

Among many other features, Microsoft Word will let you:

- Copy, move, and change the appearance of text within a document with a click of the mouse
- Create documents using ready-made templates
- Automatically add page numbers and footnotes to documents
- Automatically find and correct spelling and grammatical errors
- Include tables and charts of data or text
- Import and place graphics into your documents for added effect
- Easily create envelopes, labels, or form letters
- See how your document will appear before you print it

Microsoft Word keeps each document (letter, report, or other piece of work you create) in the computer's memory while you are working with it. In order to keep it, you have to save each document as a file on your computer's storage device (either floppy or hard disk). These documents can contain a few words or thousands of words and images.

Case Study:
Sabrina Lee, a graduating senior from Indiana University, is learning to use Microsoft Word to create a cover letter that she will include with her resume when she sends it to a prospective employer.

Starting Word

Concept

To use the Microsoft Word program, or **application**, the user must open it.

Do It!

Sabrina wants to open the Microsoft Word application so she can work on a cover letter.

1 Make sure the computer, monitor, and any other necessary peripheral devices are turned on. The Windows screen should appear on your monitor, as shown in Figure 1-1. Your screen may differ slightly from the one shown.

2 Click the [Start] button on the Windows taskbar at the bottom of your screen. This will bring up the **Windows Start** menu.

3 Move the mouse pointer ⌖ up the Start menu to the **Programs** bar to make the **Programs** menu appear. (See Figure 1-2.)

4 Position the pointer on **Microsoft Word**, highlighting it, and click to open the application. (If Word is not there, try looking under **Microsoft Office** on the Start menu.) Word will open with a blank document in the window.

More

When you started Word you may have noticed a small window containing the Office Assistant. If the Assistant is not in your Word window it can be accessed by clicking the Office Assistant button 🔘 found at the right side of the Standard toolbar. Part of the Microsoft Office Help facility, the Assistant offers tips, advice, and help on most Word functions. The Assistant has the ability to guess the help topic you desire based on the actions you are performing, and it can also answer queries by accepting full questions rather than only being limited to keyword searches. When the Assistant feels that you need help with a particular feature it will produce a light bulb in its window, or on the Office Assistant button. The Assistant will become active when you use a wizard, walking you through the steps, offering advice and suggestions. Clicking this light bulb will cause a tip to materialize in the window. Clicking on the Assistant brings up a balloon with various options, help topics, and a space in which you can type your question.

If the proper files are installed on your computer you can change the appearance of the Assistant by clicking the options button in the Assistant's balloon. The Office Assistant dialog box also offers choices for customizing the Assistant and its functionality. Clicking the close button in the Assistant's window will hide the Assistant.

Figure 1-1 Windows screen

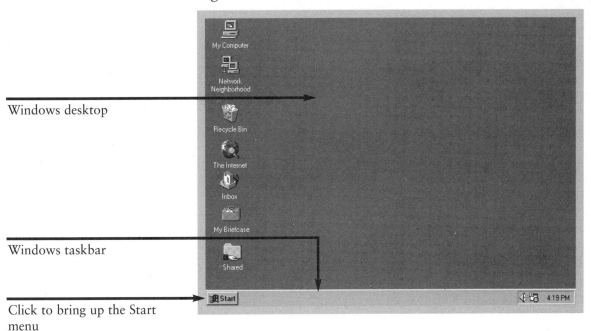

Windows desktop

Windows taskbar

Click to bring up the Start
menu

Figure 1-2 Opening Word from the Start menu

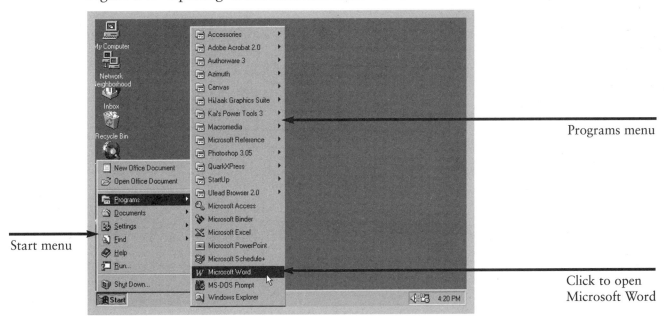

Programs menu

Start menu

Click to open
Microsoft Word

Practice

Click File, then click Exit to close Word,
then open Word again.

Hot Tip

Each computer can vary in its setup
depending on its hardware and software
configurations. Therefore, your Word start-
up procedure may be slightly different from
that described above.

Exploring
the Word Screen

Concept

When Word is opened, it will present a window with many common Windows features including title, menu, and toolbars. In addition to these, there are many features unique to Word that are designed to make document production fast, flexible, and more convenient.

The Microsoft Word screen, or **application window**, contains the following components, as shown in Figure 1-3:

The **title bar** shows the name of the application and the name of the active document. A new document is automatically called Document1, Document2, etc., until it is saved with a new name.

The **menu bar** shows the names of menus containing Word commands. Clicking on one of these names will make its menu appear, listing the commands you may choose from. Most commands available in Microsoft Word can be found here.

The **Standard toolbar** contains buttons with icons illustrating commonly used commands. When you position the mouse pointer over a button on a toolbar, the button becomes raised and a small box called a **ScreenTip** will appear below the button naming its function. Using toolbar buttons is faster than pulling down menus.

The **Formatting toolbar** contains the **Style, Font,** and **Size** boxes along with buttons for common formatting commands. You will learn about additional toolbars in later lessons.

The **horizontal ruler** shows paragraph and document margins and tab settings. In page layout view, the horizontal ruler also shows column widths and a vertical ruler appears.

The **insertion point** is the blinking vertical bar that marks the place where text will appear as it is entered.

The **document window** is the open space in which your document appears. When the mouse pointer enters the document window it changes from an arrow to an **I-beam** so you can more accurately position it in text.

The positions of the **scroll bar boxes** in the **scroll bars** show where the text on the screen is located in the document. You can move quickly through a document by clicking the **scroll bar arrows** at either end of the bars to move the scroll box, or you can click and drag the box itself. The horizontal scroll bar also contains the four **view buttons**. These allow you to view your document in different ways, which you will learn about in Lesson 3.

The left-hand section of the **status bar** tells you what page and section of your document is currently displayed and the total number of pages. The next section shows the distance (in inches) from the insertion point to the top of the page and its current position given as coordinates of Line and Column number. The remaining portion of the bar is dedicated to showing whether certain commands are currently active.

Figure 1-3 Components of the Word application window

Title bar

Menu bar

Standard toolbar

Formatting toolbar

Horizontal ruler

Insertion point

Document window

Vertical scroll bar

Office Assistant

Horizontal scroll bar

Horizontal scroll bar box

View buttons

Status bar

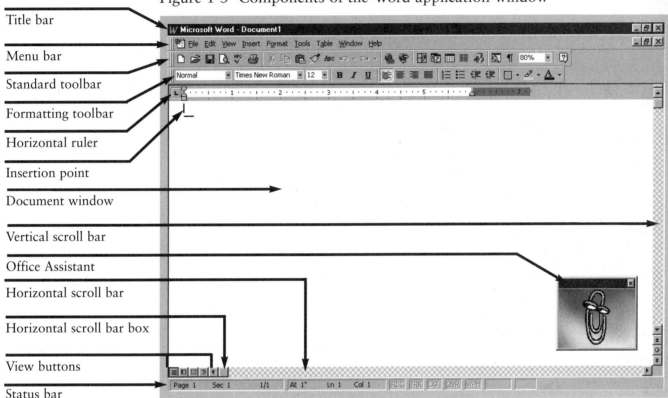

Practice

Familiarize yourself with the tools in the toolbar by positioning the mouse pointer over each button and reading its ScreenTip.

Hot Tip

Your screen may have been customized to show more or fewer toolbars, or to show them in different locations from those in the illustration. You will learn how to adjust these settings in Lesson 3.

Creating a Word Document and Entering Text

Concept

Just as a new sheet of paper must be put into a typewriter before you can type, you must create a new **document** before you can enter information into Microsoft Word.

Do It!

Sabrina wants to open a new document in Microsoft Word and enter text.

1 When you opened Word, a new document should have appeared with Document1 in the title bar. You can also create a new document once Word is open by clicking the **New document** button 🗋 on the left end of the Standard toolbar.

2 Using the blank document you just opened, type in the following address, pressing [**Enter**] after each line:

> Sabrina Lee
> 12 Oakleigh St.
> Indianapolis, IN 46202

The text will appear at the insertion point as you are typing it. When you are finished, your document should resemble Figure 1-4.

More

In this example, you pressed [**Enter**] after each line of text to begin a new one because an address consists of short, distinct lines. When writing in a document that does not require abbreviated lines, you do not have to press [**Enter**] to begin a new line, as Word uses a feature known as **word wrap** to continue on the next line when you run out of space in the line you are on. If a word is too long to be added to the end of the current line, it is placed at the beginning of the line below, allowing you to type without interruptions or guesswork.

A new document may also be made by clicking **File,** then clicking **New.** As shown in Figure 1-5, the New dialog box will appear, giving you several options to create new documents. For now you will learn to use general blank documents. Other kinds of documents and methods of document creation will be covered in Lesson 2.

You may have noticed that some words had wavy red lines beneath them. If **Automatic Spell Checking** is active, Word checks your spelling automatically as you go along and in this fashion points out words it does not recognize. These lines will not appear when the document is printed. You will find out more about Word's spell-check options in Lesson 3. You may also have noticed dots appearing in spaces and a ¶ at the end of every paragraph and blank line. These are called nonprinting characters and, as the name implies, they do not affect the final appearance of your document. Nonprinting characters can be turned on and off with the **Show/Hide ¶** button ¶ on the Standard toolbar. A ¶, or **paragraph mark**, is created every time [**Enter**] is pressed.

Figure 1-4 Sabrina's name and address

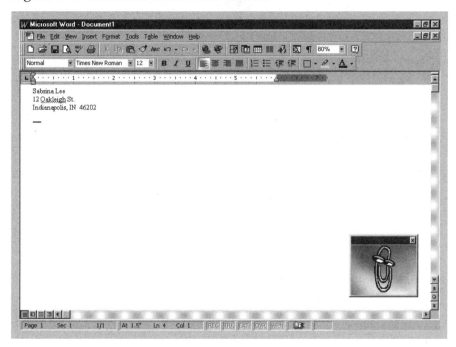

Figure 1-5 New dialog box

Standard blank document
template

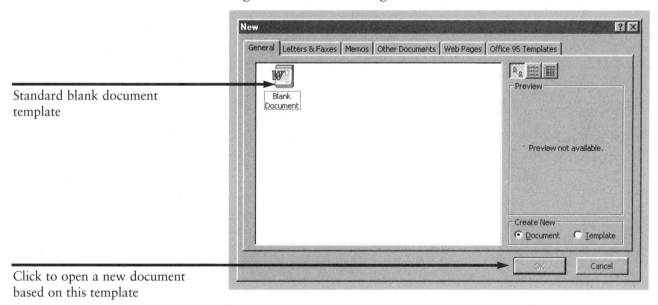

Click to open a new document
based on this template

Saving and Closing a Document

Concept

When using a computer, it is essential to **Save** documents by giving them unique names and storing them on a floppy disk or the hard drive. Otherwise, work will be lost when Word is exited or when the computer is shut down. It is also a good idea to save documents as they are modified so that work will not be lost due to power or computer failures. **Closing** a document removes it from the screen and "puts it away" until it is needed again.

Do It!

Save Sabrina's name and address as a file called **address.doc** and close it.

1 You should still have Sabrina's address on your screen from the previous Skill. Click **File**, then click **Save As** to bring up the Save As dialog box, shown in Figure 1-6. (If you had chosen the Save command, the Save As dialog box would appear anyway, as this is the first time you have saved your document.)

2 Word will automatically name your document based on its first few words. In this case, the file name (displayed in the **File name** box) is not acceptable, so you must type in another in its place. Notice that the default file name is highlighted. This selected text will be replaced when you begin to type.

3 Type the file name **Address** into the File name box. (The dialog box opens with the File name box already activated and ready to receive text.) If you choose not to add the .doc extension to the end of the file name, Word will do it for you automatically when it saves the file. An extension tells the computer what kind of file it is attached to. The extension ".doc" identifies a Word file.

4 Word needs to be told where your document should be stored in the computer. Click the **Save in** box to select a location. You will be saving it on your student disk unless your instructor tells you to save the file in a different drive and folder.

5 Click [Save] to save your document to the selected location.

6 Click **File**, then click **Close**. The document will disappear from the screen.

More

If you modify a document and do not save the changes before you close it, Word will ask you if you want to save it in one of two ways. If the Assistant is open it will prompt you to save changes via a button in its balloon. If the Assistant is not open Word will bring up a dialog box asking if you wish to save changes. These are synonymous methods of saving a file. If you do not save, any changes you have made since the last time you saved will be lost. You can create a new folder to save your document in by clicking the **Create New Folder** button 🖾 on the Save As screen. A document can also be closed by clicking the **Close** button ☒ at the right end of the menu bar. The Close button is grouped with the **sizing** buttons 🔳🔲, called the **Minimize** and **Maximize** buttons, respectively. Minimizing the document hides it and displays it as a button at the bottom of the window; it may be viewed by double-clicking it or by clicking one of its sizing buttons. When the screen is maximized, the Maximize button will be replaced with the **Restore** button 🔲, which reduces the window to its previous size. Likewise, when the screen is minimized, the Restore button will appear in place of the Minimize button. Notice there are two sets of sizing buttons. The upper set controls the application window and the lower set controls the document. Closing the application window exits Word. The sizing and Close commands are also available on the **Document Window Control** menu, which you can access by clicking the **Document Window Control** icon 🔳 in the upper left corner of the document window. The **Application Window Control** icon 🔳 performs the same functions for the application window.

Figure 1-6 Save As dialog box

Save Location

Creates a new folder in which to save the file

Commands and settings

Practice

Save the document to your student disk again, this time as **address2.doc**.

Hot Tip

You can save a Word file as a Web page by selecting the Save as HTML command from the File menu. When you save as a Web page, Word closes the file and then reopens it in HTML format.

Opening an Existing Document

Concept

To view or edit a document that is saved in the computer, the user must first open it.

Do It!

Sabrina needs to open her updated cover letter. The file is saved under the name **Doit1-6.doc**.

1 Click **File**, then click **Open**. The Open dialog box will appear, letting you choose which document to open.

2 Click the **Look in** box to select which drive your document is in. A list of folders and documents will appear, as shown in Figure 1-7. The drives, files, and directories on your screen may be different from those in the figure. Clicking on a drive or folder will list what documents or folders it contains. Double-clicking documents or folders will open them. Ask your instructor where to locate the appropriate student files.

3 Click **Doit1-6** to select it. It will appear highlighted.

4 Click [Open] to open the file.

More

Word can open word processing documents in almost any file format. That is, files created with other programs can be opened and edited by Word. To open a file of a different format from the Open dialog box, just click the **Files of type** box and click **All Files** (*.*). This causes all files to appear in the box above it, available for opening.

Figure 1-7 Open dialog box

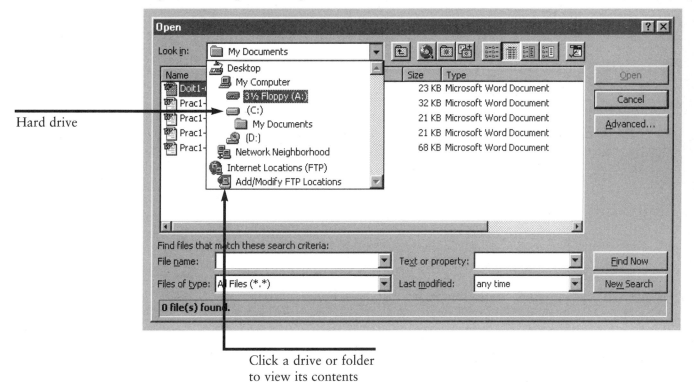

Hard drive

Click a drive or folder
to view its contents

Deleting and Inserting Text

Concept

One of the fundamental advantages of word processing is the ease it provides in changing what has been previously entered. Word makes it easy to replace or delete unwanted text.

Do It!

Sabrina wants to modify her address by changing "Oakleigh St." to "Oakleigh Street."

1 Make sure that **Doit1-6** (which was opened in the previous Skill) is still in the active window.

2 Move the **insertion point** to the immediate right of the period in "St." in Sabrina's address by moving the mouse pointer there and clicking.

3 Press [**Backspace**] once to erase the period.

4 Enter **r-e-e-t** to correct the address. Sabrina's address should resemble the one at the bottom of Figure 1-8.

5 Save the file to your student disk as **Letter.doc**.

More

As you just saw, the [Backspace] key erases the character immediately to the left of the insertion point. To erase the character to the right of the insertion point, press [**Delete**]. Word inserts text at the insertion point; that is, it moves nearby text to the right instead of typing over it. To type over existing text without moving it, double-click the **Overtype** button OVR on the status bar to enter Overtype mode.

You can move the insertion point one character at a time to the left or right and one line at a time up or down with the **arrow keys** on the keyboard. This is especially helpful when you are moving the insertion point only a short distance. More ways to move the insertion point using the keyboard are shown in Table 1-1. If you will be using the [**Home**], [**End**], [**Pg Up**], and [**Pg Dn**] keys on the numeric keypad, as required for some of the movement techniques in the table, you must first make sure that **Num Lock** is disabled. Some keyboards include separate keys for these functions.

Figure 1-8 Changing "St." to "Street" in Sabrina's address

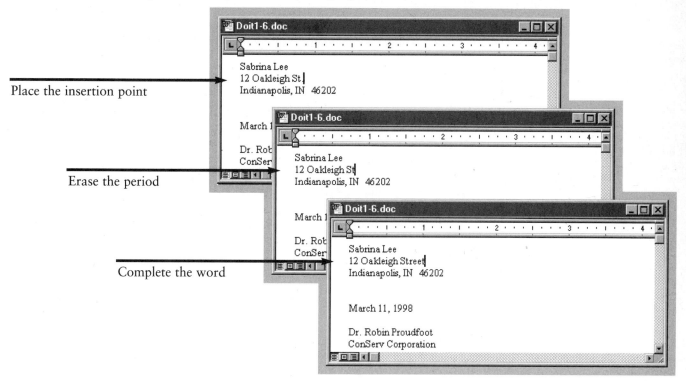

Place the insertion point

Erase the period

Complete the word

Table 1-1   Moving the Insertion Point with the Keyboard

To move the insertion point	Press
Left or right one word	[Ctrl]+[←] or [Ctrl]+[→]
Up or down one paragraph	[Ctrl]+[↑] or [Ctrl]+[↓]
Up or down one screen	[Pg Up] or [Pg Dn]
To the beginning or end of a line	[Home] or [End]
To the beginning or end of a document	[Ctrl]+[Home] or [Ctrl]+[End]

Practice

To practice deleting and modifying text, open the student file **Prac1-7**.

Hot Tip

The **Undo** button ⟲ on the Standard tool-bar allows you to take back the last command you used.

Formatting Text

Concept

Word allows the user to easily change the **font, font size,** and **alignment** of text in a document in addition to several other formatting options.

Do It!

Sabrina wants to make her name bold and change the font size of her document.

1 Make sure that **Letter.doc** is still in the active window.

2 **Select** Sabrina's name by clicking before the **S** in Sabrina and dragging (moving the mouse with the button held down) to the end of her last name. The selected text will appear white-on-black.

3 Click the **Bold** button **B** on the **Formatting** toolbar. The letters in her name will appear thicker.

4 **Deselect** the text by clicking once anywhere in the document window.

5 **Select** the entire document by clicking before the **S** in Sabrina and dragging down to after the period in "**…enc.**" at the end of the document.

6 Click the **Font Size** arrow 10 ▼ on the Formatting toolbar and then click **11**. (See Figure 1-9.) The text in the document will increase slightly in size. Do not close the document, as you will be using it in the next Skill.

More

There are several attributes of text that the Formatting toolbar allows you to work with. The **Font** or typeface refers to the actual shape of each individual letter or number as it appears on the screen or in a printed document. Text **Size** is usually measured in **points**. For example, the text in a newspaper is ordinarily printed in 10 point. Sabrina changed her name to 11 point from Word's default of 10. Other formatting options available include **Bold** **B** , **Italic** **I** , **Underline** **U** , and **Highlight** . **Alignment** refers to the manner in which text follows the margins of your document. (See Figure 1-10.) Knowing how to format text for maximum effect is an essential skill that will make your documents appear crisp and professional. Notice how the text on this page is used; different fonts and sizes are used for headings and subject matter, and important terms are bold for added emphasis. To format an entire document, as above, you must select it first. You can select an entire document without dragging the mouse pointer over it by clicking **Edit**, then clicking **Select All**. You can also change the color of your font by clicking the **Font Color** button and then selecting a color of your choice.

Figure 1-9 Adjusting font size

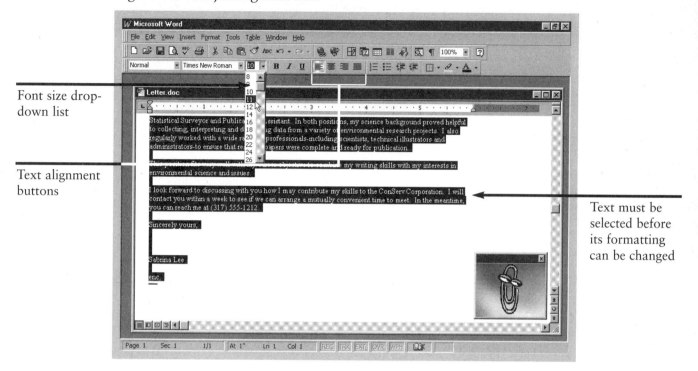

Font size drop-down list

Text alignment buttons

Text must be selected before its formatting can be changed

Figure 1-10 Text alignment

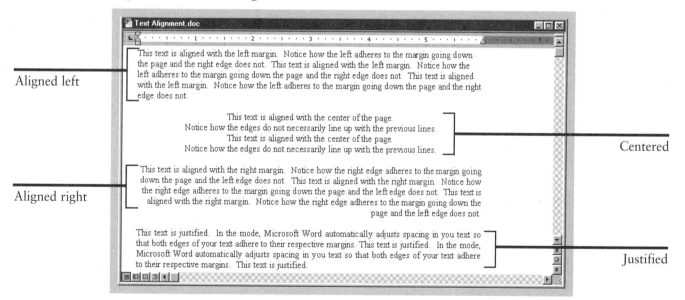

Aligned left

Centered

Aligned right

Justified

To practice formatting text, open the student file **Prac1-8**.

You will learn several more text selection techniques in Lesson 2.

Printing a Document

Concept

If the computer is properly connected to a printer, a document can be **printed** with the click of a button. Or, if more flexibility in printing is desired, Word provides more comprehensive options, including a **Print Preview** that allows the user to see the document as it will appear when printed.

Do It!

Sabrina wants to print her document.

1 Make sure your computer is properly connected to a printer. (Ask your instructor.)

2 Click **File**, then click **Print** to bring up the Print dialog box (Figure 1-11).

3 Click [OK] to print. (Clicking the Print button 🖨 on the Standard toolbar skips the dialog box and prints automatically.)

4 Save and close the document.

More

You can also view your document as it will appear when printed by clicking **File**, then clicking **Print Preview**. The Print Preview screen (Figure 1-12) will come up, a miniature version of your document will appear, and the mouse pointer will change to the **magnification tool** 🔍 when it is in the document window. The Standard and Formatting toolbars are replaced with the **Print Preview** toolbar, and the vertical ruler appears. The **Zoom Control** selection box displays how much the document has been shrunk or magnified. To view a particular portion of your document up close, simply click it to display it at 100%, of normal size. The mouse pointer will then change to 🔍 and clicking will reverse the magnification. To edit in magnification mode, click the **Magnifier** button 🔍 to change the mouse pointer to an I-beam, then edit and enter text as you normally would. When you are finished editing, click the Magnifier button again to look at other parts of the document. If the document appears correct, you can print it by clicking the Print button at the left end of the Print Preview toolbar. To exit the Print Preview screen and return to your document, click [Close].

Figure 1-11 Print dialog box

Specify your
printer type here

Additional printer
options

Prints only the
page where the
mouse pointer
currently is

Click to increase
number of copies

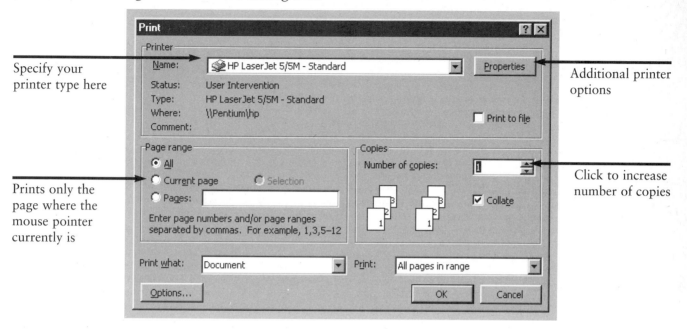

Figure 1-12 Print Preview screen

Magnifier button

Print Preview
toolbar

Magnification
level on screen

Click with this
pointer (the
Magnification
tool) to examine
the document
more closely

Preview of how
document will
appear when
printed

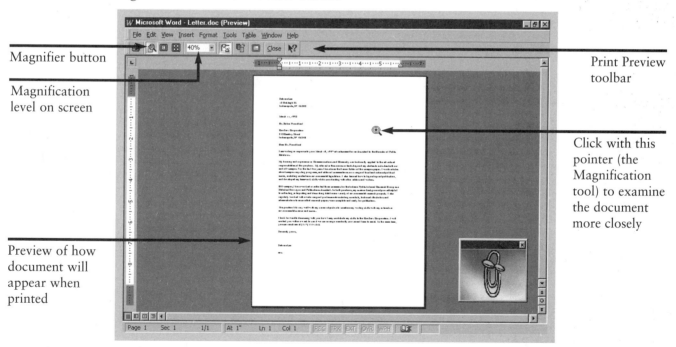

Practice

To practice previewing a document, open
the student file **Prac1-9**.

Hot Tip

The Print Preview screen is a **WYSIWYG**
(What You See Is What You Get, pronoun-
ced "wizzy-wig") display, meaning that
what appears on the screen is what will
print out in the final copy.

Shortcuts

Function	Button/Mouse	Menu	Keyboard
Create a new document	🗋	Click File, then click New	[Ctrl]+[N]
Show/Hide nonprinting characters	¶	Click Tools, then click Options, then click the View tab; Choose All	[Ctrl]+[Shift]+[*]
Save the active document	🖫	Click File, then click Save	[Ctrl]+[S]
Close the active document	⊠	Click the control menu icon, then click Close	[Alt]+[F4]
Maximize the active document window	▢	Click the control menu icon, then click Maximize	[Alt]+[F10]
Minimize the active document window	▬	Click the control menu icon, then click Minimize	
Restore the active document window to its previous size	🗗	Click the control menu icon, then click Restore	
Open a document	📂	Click File, then click Open	[Ctrl]+[O]
Bold selected text	**B**	Click Format, then click Font; Choose Bold	[Ctrl]+[B]
Italicize selected text	*I*	Click Format, then click Font; Choose Italic	[Ctrl]+[I]
Underline selected text	U̲	Click Format, then click Font; Choose Underline	[Ctrl]+[U]
Highlight selected text	🖊		
Print Preview	🔍	Click File, then click Print Preview	
Print the active document	🖨	Click File, then click Print	[Ctrl]+[P]

Identify Key Features

Figure 1-13 Identifying components of the Word screen

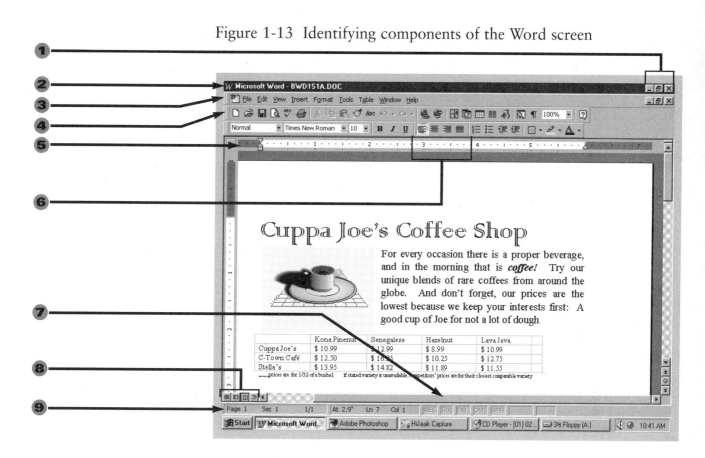

Select the Best Answer

10. The exact location where text appears when entered

11. The shape of letters and numbers

12. Reduces a window to a button on the Windows Taskbar

13. The way in which text relates to the left and right margins

14. A window that appears allowing access to specialized commands

15. Allows you to see how your document will appear when printed

a. Minimize button

b. Alignment

c. Print Preview screen

d. Insertion point

e. Font

f. Dialog box

Quiz (continued)

Complete the Statement

16. In order to change the formatting of a section of text, you must first:

    a. Click one of the formatting buttons

    b. Save the document

    c. Select the text to be changed

    d. Click the Start button

17. Clicking the 🖫 button:

    a. Ejects the floppy disk

    b. Saves the document

    c. Searches for a file on the hard drive

    d. Selects text

18. Clicking the 🔍 button on the Standard toolbar:

    a. Searches the document for errors

    b. Magnifies part of the document

    c. Opens the Print Preview window

    d. Brings up the Document Detective window

19. An ellipsis (...) after a command in the command menu means that:

    a. That command has a dialog box

    b. That command is unavailable

    c. The shortcut for that command is the [...] key

    d. The whole name could not fit on the menu

20. The elements of text formatting do NOT include:

    a. Font size

    b. Justification

    c. Style

    d. Delete

21. Text that is justified is:

    a. Carefully edited

    b. Adjusted to meet both margins

    c. Centered

    d. Righteous!

Interactivity

Test Your Skills

1. Identify a job that interests you and determine what the employer is looking for:

   a. Go to the classified section of a newspaper or to an online job listing and find a specific listing that you think might suit you.

   b. Think about what skills and experience might be necessary to successfully apply. You may wish to call the employer or agency in the advertisement to identify more precisely the qualifications of the job.

2. Open Word and write a brief letter applying for the job:

   a. Launch Word using the Start menu.

   b. Enter your name and address at the top of the page.

   c. Skip a line and enter the address and name (if available) of the prospective employer.

   d. Skip a line and enter today's date.

   e. Write the body of the letter, beginning with a salutation and continuing with four short paragraphs, one each for your educational background, prior job experience, any other relevant experience, and the reasons for your interest in this particular job.

3. Format the letter text to more effectively present the letter.

   a. Make all the text in the letter 12 pt Times New Roman.

   b. Bold your name at the top of the letter.

   c. Align your name and address with the right margin by selecting the appropriate lines and clicking the Align Right button on the Formatting toolbar.

4. Print the letter, then save and close the document and exit Word.

   a. After making sure your computer is properly connected to a working printer, click the Print button on the Standard toolbar to print the letter.

   b. Save the letter to your student disk as **Test 1**.

   c. Close the document and exit Word by clicking the application Close button at the right end of the title bar.

Interactivity (continued)

Problem Solving

Using the skills you learned in Lesson 1, open a new document and write your name, address, and today's date on it as a heading, then add a few sentences about yourself. Then adjust its formatting so that it matches the example in Figure 1-14 below. Then conduct a print preview to check it and print it. Save it on your student disk as **Solved 1**.

Figure 1-14 Problem Solving

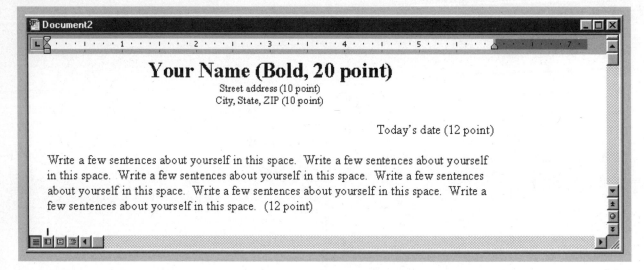

L E S S O N

2

EDITING DOCUMENTS

Once text has been entered into a Word document, it may be manipulated and edited to suit the requirements of the user. Text may be selected in several different ways so that particular portions can be modified without affecting the rest of the document. Selected text can be copied or moved, or it may be deleted altogether.

Word has a powerful file search function that allows the user to find documents based on a wide variety of search criteria, and a help facility that provides many kinds of information and assistance with various word processing tasks and special features of Word.

In addition to the general blank document template on which Word bases its standard new document, there are a multitude of other templates for document types that can be created with Word. There are also programs called wizards that guide the user through the steps necessary to create various complex documents.

Case Study:
In this lesson, Sabrina will edit her cover letter and create a résumé to go with it, as well as search for a document and explore Word's help facility.

Skill   Searching for Files

Concept

There are so many locations in a computer's storage devices in which data may be saved that documents are sometimes difficult to locate. Word's Open dialog box contains **powerful search tools** to locate and open misplaced files.

Do It!

Sabrina would like to open the Windows Frequently Asked Questions (FAQ) file, but she doesn't know where it is located.

1 Click the **Open** button on the Standard toolbar. The Open dialog box appears, as shown in Figure 2-1. Now you must set the parameters of your search.

2 Click the **Look in** list arrow, then click the **C:** drive. This confines the search to your primary hard drive.

3 Click on the **File name** text box to place the insertion point there, and type **FAQ** in it. That is the name of the file you are searching for.

4 Click the **Files of type** list arrow and select **Unicode Text Files (*.txt)**.

5 Click the **Commands and Settings** button , then click **Search Subfolders**. Thus, instead of searching for your file name only among the parent folders in your chosen drive, the computer will also search within the subfolders they contain for files bearing the chosen name. When the computer has completed its search, **faq.txt** should be selected, and Word will display a file hierarchy showing the location of the file in the computer's memory.

6 Press [**Enter**] to open the selected item. Word will open the text file, which contains a troubleshooting guide for Windows.

7 Close the document when you are finished with it. Do not save changes.

More

Word's search abilities are immense. The **Text or property** text box allows you to search for documents containing specific words or characters by entering the text fragment in the Text or property text box within quotation marks. Without quotation marks Word will search for documents whose Properties dialog box contains the entered text. The **Last modified** text box lets you restrict the search to documents modified yesterday, last week, and so on.

If you are connected to an internet provider, you can search the Web by clicking the Search the Web button . Clicking this button calls up your Web browser and takes you to a search page. By searching the Web by topic or keyword, a search engine will provide you with an organized list of links to relevant Web sites. There is also a Web toolbar that contains the Search the Web button, as well as providing a text box in which you can specify a URL that you would like to go to.

Figure 2-1 Searching for a file from the Open dialog box

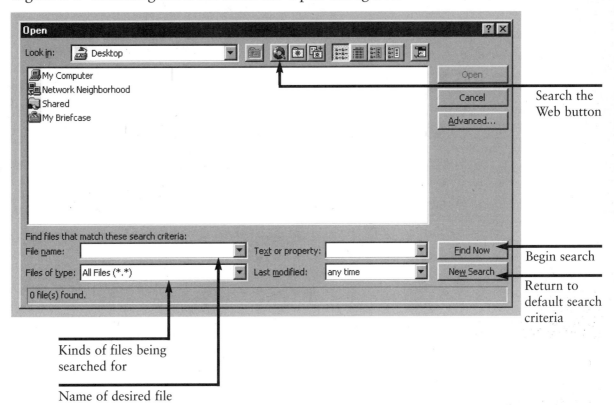

Search the
Web button

Begin search

Return to
default search
criteria

Kinds of files being
searched for

Name of desired file

Practice

To practice finding files in Word, open the
student file **Prac2-1**.

Hot Tip

Being as restrictive as possible in your
search criteria will make the search process
faster and reduce the number of unwanted
files found.

Selecting Text and Undoing Actions

Concept

Sections of text must be **selected** before they can be modified. Selecting text causes the selected area to act as a single unit that can moved, modified, or formatted. Text that is selected appears highlighted on the screen. That is, text that is normally black on a white screen will appear white on a black background. The **Undo** command can be used to correct errors by reversing previous commands or actions.

Do It!

Sabrina wants to select a paragraph using two different selection methods.

1. Open the student file **Doit2-2** and save it to your student disk as **Cover Letter**.

2. Scroll down to the paragraph that begins, "My training and experience...."

3. **Select** the paragraph by clicking just before the first letter and dragging the mouse pointer to the end of the paragraph. If the Office Assistant is in the way it will automatically move to another location.

4. Type the letter **X**. The selected text will be replaced by the text you entered.

5. Click the **Undo** button ⟲ on the Standard toolbar to bring back the missing paragraph.

6. Deselect the paragraph by clicking once anywhere in the document window.

7. Now select the same paragraph by **triple-clicking** any portion of it.

More

Once text is selected, it can be replaced by typing in new text; the new entry will take the place of what was selected. When clicking and dragging to select text, the selected area will follow the mouse pointer letter by letter in the first word; subsequent words will be added to the selected area all at once. To select a single line or multiple lines of text, use the **selection bar**, a column of space beneath the 🅛 in the horizontal ruler. (See Figure 2-2.) When the mouse pointer enters this area, it will appear reversed ⳤ, and clicking will select the entire line to its right. Dragging up or down will select additional lines. More ways to select text are shown in Tables 2-1 and 2-2. Keep in mind that Num Lock must be disabled in order to use the [Home], [End], and arrow keys on the numeric keypad.

You can select large sections of text by placing the insertion point at the beginning, moving to the other end, and pressing [**Shift**] while you click there.

The Undo command is an essential tool that easily corrects many of the worst mistakes you will make when using Word. The Undo and Redo buttons are grouped on the Standard toolbar. Clicking the **Undo** drop-down list arrow ⟲⁻ brings down the Undo drop-down list, which lets you undo one or more of several recently completed actions and commands by simply clicking on the item you wish to undo. The Redo command and its drop-down list work in a similar fashion, but instead reverse past Undo commands.

Figure 2-2 Selection bar

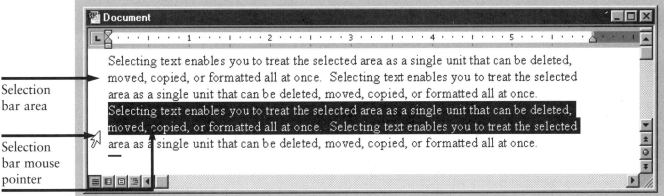

Selection
bar area

Selection
bar mouse
pointer

Selected
text

Table 2-1   Mouse Selection Shortcuts

Desired Selection	Action to Take
A single word	Double-click the word
A sentence	Click the sentence while pressing [Ctrl]
A paragraph	Triple-click the paragraph or double-click next to it in the selection bar
A line of text	Click next to it in the selection bar
A vertical block of text	Click and drag while pressing [Alt]
The entire document	Triple-click in the selection bar

Table 2-2   Keyboard Selection Shortcuts

Desired Selection	Action to take
A single character	[Shift]+[←] or [Shift]+[→]
A single word	[Ctrl]+[Shift]+[←] or [Ctrl]+[Shift]+[→]
A paragraph	[Ctrl]+[Shift]+[↑] or [Ctrl]+[Shift]+[↓]
To the beginning or end of a line	[Shift]+[Home] or [Shift]+[End]
To the beginning or end of a document	[Ctrl]+[Shift]+[Home] or [Ctrl]+[Shift]+[End]
A vertical block of text	[Ctrl]+[Shift]+[F8] and move with arrow keys
The entire document (Select All)	[Ctrl]+[A]

Practice

To practice selecting text and using the Undo command, open the student file **Prac2-2**.

Hot Tip

When you choose an action to undo from the Undo drop-down list, all actions that took place after the selected action will be undone as well.

 # Cutting, Copying, and Moving Text

---

Concept

Sections of text can be easily moved within a Word document, deleted or copied from one place and reapplied in another. Word offers two ways to move text: the **drag-and-drop** method, which uses the mouse and will be discussed in the next Skill; and **cut-and-paste**, which uses the **Windows Clipboard**.

Do It!

Sabrina wants to move a paragraph in her cover letter using the Cut-and-Paste method.

1 **Select** the entire paragraph that begins with "This position...," as shown in Figure 2-3. (The file **Cover Letter** should still be in the active window.)

2 Click the **Cut** button ✂ on the Standard toolbar. The selected text disappears, leaving an extra blank line between the remaining paragraphs.

3 Press [**Backspace**] once to remove the extra blank line.

4 Place the insertion point to the left of the first letter in the second paragraph in the message section, the one that begins, "My training and experience...."

5 Click the **Paste** button 📋 on the Standard toolbar. The text you cut earlier reappears at the insertion point.

6 Press [**Enter**] to add a blank line to separate the paragraphs.

7 Close the file, saving changes if prompted.

More

The Cut, Copy, and Paste commands use the **Windows Clipboard**, a temporary holding area for data. The Cut command removes selected data to the Clipboard, while the Copy command leaves selected text where it is and sends a copy of it to the Clipboard. The Paste command inserts data stored in the Clipboard at the insertion point. The Clipboard can also be used to move data between documents or even between different programs, such as a paint program and a spreadsheet. The Clipboard stores only one item of data at a time, whether text or graphic, and each time a new item is cut or copied it replaces the previous contents of the Clipboard. The Cut, Copy, and Paste commands are also available on the Edit menu.

Figure 2-3 Selected paragraph

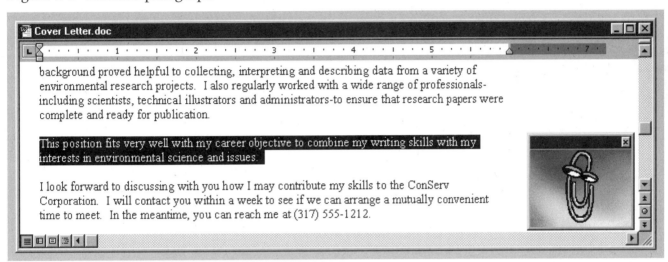

Practice

To practice cutting, copying, and pasting text, open the student file **Prac2-3**.

Hot Tip

Though pressing [Delete] removes selected text just as using the Cut command does, it does not save it to the Clipboard, and thus the text cannot be reinserted elsewhere.

 # Copying and Moving Text with the Mouse

Concept

The **drag-and-drop** method of copying and moving text is quick and convenient for moving text a short distance within a Word document. In many instances it is preferable to using the Clipboard with the Cut, Copy, and Paste commands.

Do It!

Sabrina wants to move a paragraph in her cover letter using the drag-and-drop method.

1 Open the student file **Doit2-4** and save it to your student disk as **Cover Letter 2**.

2 Select the entire paragraph that begins with "This position" including the blank line beneath it, as shown in Figure 2-4.

3 Click on a portion of the selected area without releasing the mouse button. The mouse pointer will change into the **drag-and-drop** pointer, indicating that there is text loaded and ready to be inserted.

4 Position the dotted insertion point to the left of the first letter in the second paragraph in the message section, the one that begins, "My training and experience...."

5 Release the mouse button. The text will disappear from its previous location and reappear at the insertion point.

More

Dragging and dropping text moves it from its previous location. To copy the text to another area while leaving the original intact, press [**Ctrl**] before dropping the dragged text. The drag-and-drop pointer will appear with a small plus in a box at the bottom to signify that it will make a copy of the selected text. When the mouse button is released, the selected text will appear in its original place as well as at the insertion point.

Figure 2-4 Moving text with the mouse

Selected text will be inserted here

Drag-and-drop pointer indicating that text is being moved

Selected text that will be moved

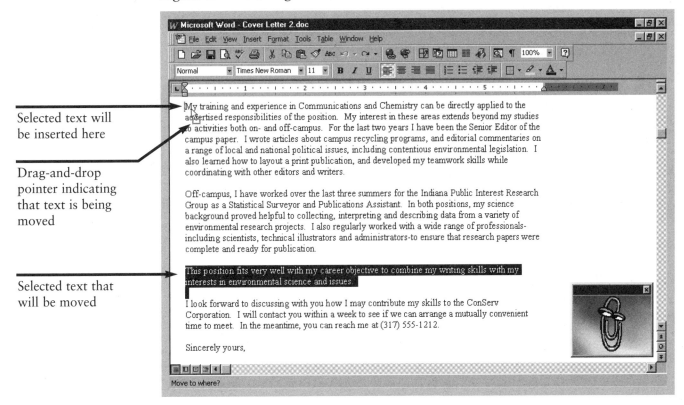

Practice

To practice copying and moving text using the mouse, open the student file **Prac2-4.**

Hot Tip

You can turn drag-and-drop text editing on and off from the Edit tab of the Options dialog box, available on the Tools menu.

 # Using the Office Assistant

Concept

The Office Assistant provides several methods for getting help in Word. You can choose from a list of topics that the assistant suggests based on the most recent functions you have performed. You can view tips related to your current activity. Or, you can ask a question in plain English.

Do It!

Sabrina wants to ask the Office Assistant about using ScreenTips.

1 Click the Office Assistant. A balloon will pop up with suggested topics related to the actions you have most recently completed.

2 In the text box type **What are ScreenTips?**, then click **Search**. The Office Assistant peruses the Word Help files and presents a selection of topics (Figure 2-5) relating to your question.

3 Position the pointer over the second bullet "Show or hide toolbar ScreenTips," the bullet will glow, and click. A window will appear, as shown in Figure 2-6, displaying the help topic.

4 Read the help topic's explanation. You can have the window on-screen to refer to while you work. When you are finished reading about ScreenTips, click the help window's close button to remove it from the screen.

More

From time to time the assistant will offer you tips on how to use Word more efficiently. The appearance of a small light bulb, either in the assistant's window or on the Office Assistant button, indicates that there is a tip to be viewed. To see the tip, just click the light bulb or Office Assistant button if the assistant is closed.

The Office Assistant can be customized. Clicking (⊙ Options) opens the Office Assistant dialog box. This dialog box has two tabs: Gallery and Options. The Gallery tab contains nine assistants you can choose from, and scrolling through the characters provides you with a preview of each one. From the Options tab, shown in Figure 2-7, you can select the Assistant's capabilities and decide what it will show tips about.

Figure 2-5 ScreenTip help topics

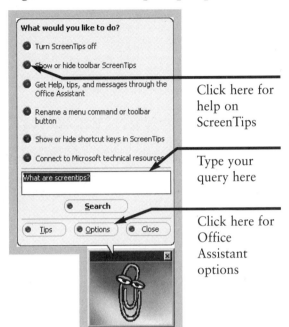

Click here for
help on
ScreenTips

Type your
query here

Click here for
Office
Assistant
options

Figure 2-6 Help on ScreenTips

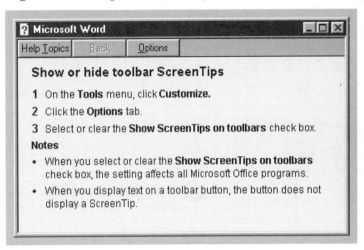

Figure 2-7 Office Assistant dialog box

This option defines F1 as
the Office Assistant hot
key

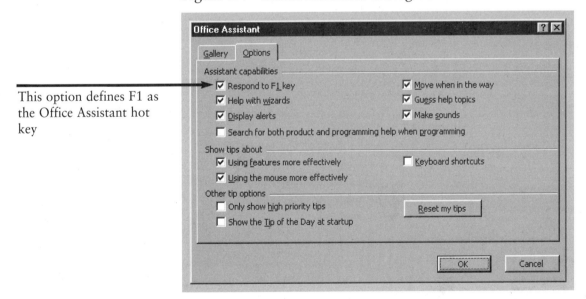

Practice

Use the Office Assistant's ability to answer
questions to get help on using the Office
Assistant.

Hot Tip

The Office Assistant is common to all
Office 97 applications. Therefore, any of
the assistant's options that you change will
affect it in all Office programs.

Getting Help in Word

Concept

Word has more traditional help facilities that are easily searched if you know what you are looking for. The Help menu contains a Contents feature which organizes information into groups, and an Index that lists all help topics alphabetically.

Do It!

Sabrina needs to use Word's Help facilities to get information about the Open command and the status bar.

1 Click **Help**, then click **What's This?** The pointer will now appear with a question mark ↳? indicating that help has been activated.

2 Click the **Open** button 📂 with the modified mouse pointer. A box called a **ScreenTip** will appear describing the command.

3 Click **Help**, then click **Contents and Index**. The Help Topics: Microsoft Word dialog box appears, as shown in Figure 2-8.

4 Click the Index tab to bring it to the front of the stack.

5 Type **status**. The list of index entries will scroll along as you type and stop on **status bar**.

6 Click ▢ Display ▢. Word searches its Help files and then opens a window (Figure 2-9) that contains information that describes that status bar and its features.

7 When you have finished reading about Word's status bar, close the Help window that Word opened.

More

If a dialog box is open, you can activate ScreenTips by clicking the help button ▢? in the upper right corner of the box. For more detailed Help, the Online Index and Contents provide comprehensive instructions and information to aid you in your work. If you know what you're looking for, the index provides an easy way to access information about various parts of Word. It lists all Help topics alphabetically and anticipates your selection as you type. Some topics open Help windows with descriptions of a Word feature when selected; others (such as the one used in the Practice file that follows) open a visual interface that lets you click on various related items to receive information about them. Still others offer animated sequences that demonstrate how to accomplish specific operations. Getting help can be difficult, however, if you are unsure of what to call your task. This is when the Office Assistant is most helpful.

Figure 2-8 Help Topics dialog box

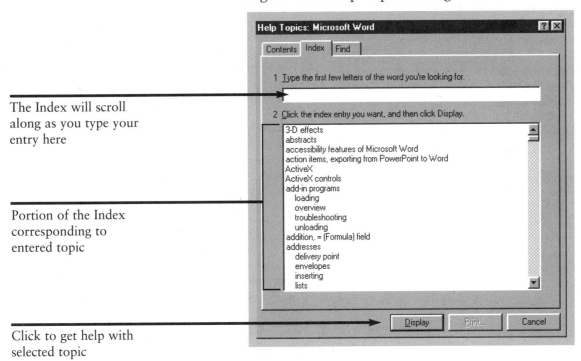

The Index will scroll along as you type your entry here

Portion of the Index corresponding to entered topic

Click to get help with selected topic

Figure 2-9 Status bar features

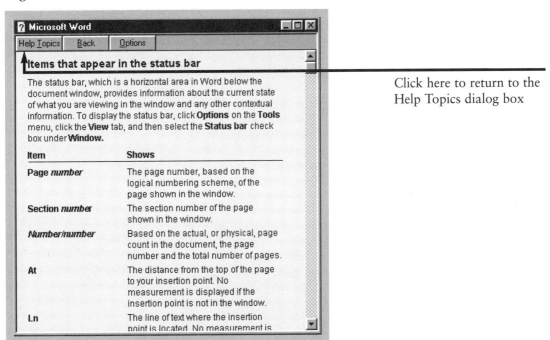

Click here to return to the Help Topics dialog box

Practice

To practice getting help in Word, open the student file **Prac2-5**.

Hot Tip

You can get help from the Microsoft Web site by selecting a command from the Microsoft on the Web submenu found on the Help menu on the Standard toolbar.

Using Templates and Wizards

Concept

When a new document is created, its font and text layout characteristics are based on a collection of previously saved settings. Together, the settings associated with this document are called a **template**. Word provides templates in many styles to choose from. When you opened Word, the new document that appeared was based on the **Blank Document** template, also known as the **Normal** template. A **wizard** is a template that walks the user through the creation of a specific type of document, such as a résumé or newsletter, further automating the process. Documents created with these tools may be freely edited and changed to meet a user's specifications.

Do It!

Sabrina wants to create a résumé with the Résumé Wizard.

1. Click **File**, then click **New** to bring up the New dialog box.

2. Click the **Other Documents** tab to bring it to the front. Several icons representing various templates and wizards appear.

3. Click the **Résumé Wizard.wiz** icon. A preview of its layout will appear in the **Preview** box, as shown in Figure 2-10.

4. Click [OK] to open the Résumé Wizard. The Résumé Wizard dialog box will appear at the Start step, as shown in Figure 2-11. The green square next to Start indicates which step of the wizard you are currently on.

5. Click [Next >] to advance to the Style step.

6. Click the **Elegant** radio button to select this style of résumé, then click [Next >].

7. At the Type step click [Next >] to use the default résumé type and advance to the next phase in the wizard. The following step allows you to enter your name, address, phone and fax numbers, and e-mail address. Word automatically enters the name of the registered user in the name text box.

8. Enter Sabrina Lee, 12 Oakleigh St., Indianapolis, IN 46202 in the name and address text boxes respectively, and delete any extraneous information that may be entered. Your Résumé Wizard text boxes should resemble those in Figure 2-12. Then click [Next >].

Figure 2-10 Templates and wizards in the New dialog box

Other tabs containing other templates and wizards

Note:
Your installation of Microsoft Word may include a different selection of templates and wizards to choose from

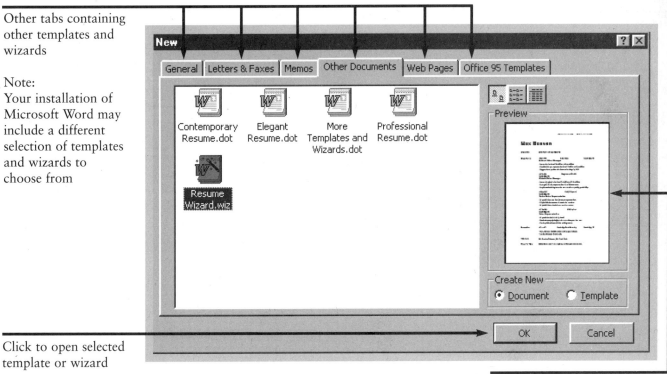

Click to open selected template or wizard

Thumbnail sketch of selected template or wizard

Figure 2-11 Résumé Wizard: Start

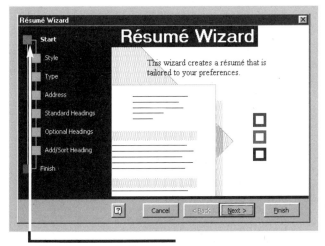

Green square indicates which step of the wizard you are on

Figure 2-12 Résumé Wizard: Address

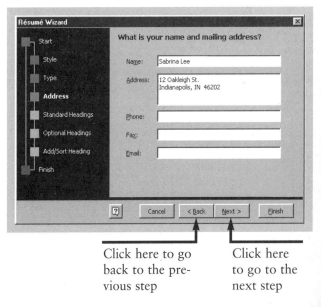

Click here to go back to the previous step

Click here to go to the next step

 **Using Templates and Wizards** (continued)

Do It!

9 At the Standard Headings step, click the interests and activities check box to add this heading to your résumé, then click Next > .

10 No additional headings will be added to your résumé; click Next > to advance the wizard.

11 The add/sort headings step allows you to insert a heading that was not included in the wizard's choices, delete a heading that you decide you do not wish to include on your résumé, or change the order or appearance of any selected headings. Click **Work experience** to select it, then click Move Up to place it before Interests and activities in your résumé, as shown in Figure 2-13. Then click Next > .

12 On the outline of the wizard's steps, at the left side of the dialog box, click the box next to **style** to go back to that step.

13 Click the Contemporary radio button to use this style rather than the previously selected Elegant, then click Finish . A résumé will appear in Page Layout view with instructions and space to fill in the rest of the necessary details, and the assistant will open, as shown in Figure 2-14, asking if you would like to do more with your résumé.

14 Click ⊘ Cancel , then close the document when you are finished viewing it.

More

Templates vary in the type and amount of formatting information that they contain. Some look like finished documents because Word inserts **Placeholders**, or text used to show you where to correctly place specific kinds of information. To add text to these templates, simply select the text you want to replace and type in your own. Other templates, such as the Professional Report template, contain less preformatting, instead offering instructions on how to use the template to create the various elements of your document. And wizards, as shown above, automate document production by asking you questions in dialog boxes. By answering these questions, you make the decisions necessary to create the document, and the wizard inserts the information and formats it automatically. Some wizards even include premade examples, in which you need only change certain text variables such as names and addresses to complete the document. Below the Preview box in the New dialog box are two radio buttons that allow you either to create a document based on a template or to directly alter a template's settings. You can create or alter a template and then save the new template to be used for future documents.

Figure 2-13 Résumé Wizard: Add/Sort Heading

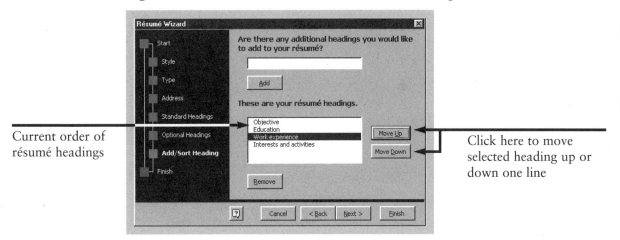

Current order of
résumé headings

Click here to move
selected heading up or
down one line

Figure 2-14 Completed résumé

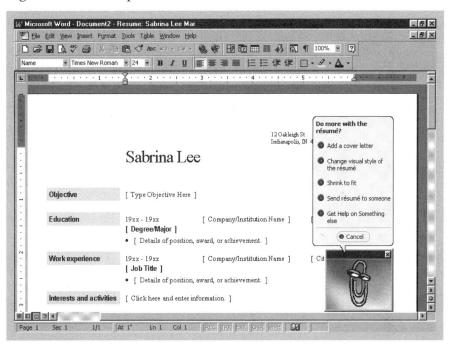

Practice

To practice using a template to create a
document, open the student file **Prac2-6**.

Hot Tip

Pressing [Ctrl]+[N] or clicking the New button automatically creates a document
based on the Normal template. You must
click the File menu and then click New in
order to access the New dialog box and the
templates and wizards that it contains.

Shortcuts

Function	Button/Mouse	Menu	Keyboard
Undo last action	↺	Click Edit, then click Undo	[Ctrl]+[Z]
Redo last undone action	↻	Click Edit, then click Redo	[Ctrl]+[Y]
Cut a selection and place it on the Clipboard	✂	Click Edit, then click Cut	[Ctrl]+[X]
Copy a selection and place the copy on the Clipboard	📋	Click Edit, then click Copy	[Ctrl]+[C]
Paste the contents of the Clipboard into the active document	📋	Click Edit, then click Paste	[Ctrl]+[V]
Call up the Office Assistant	?	Click Help, then Click Microsoft Word Help	[F1]
Get a ScreenTip for an item		Click Help, then click What's This?, then click item	[Shift]+[F1], then click item

Identify Key Features

Figure 2-15 Identifying file search features

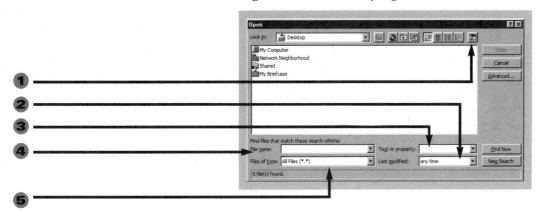

Figure 2-16 Identifying components of the Index

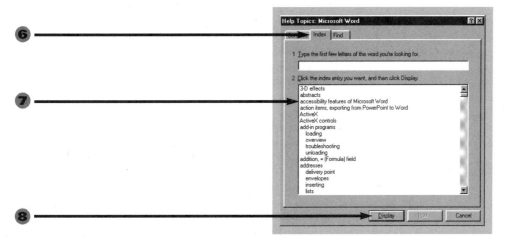

Select the Best Answer

9. An invisible column along the left edge of the text on a page

10. A command that instructs Word to look more thoroughly for a file

11. A menu of recently used commands and actions

12. Observes your work and offers suggestions

13. A program that walks you through the steps of document creation

14. Selects a paragraph

a. Drag-and-drop

b. Triple-clicking text

c. Search Subfolders

d. Wizard

e. Selection Bar

f. Undo drop-down list

Quiz (continued)

Complete the Statement

15. The dialog box where Word's file-searching capabilities are used is:

    a. The Finder dialog box

    b. The Open dialog box

    c. The Save As dialog box

    d. The Cross-reference dialog box

16. Word bases the formatting of a new document on:

    a. The last document used

    b. The buttons on the Formatting toolbar

    c. The Blank Document template

    d. The Résumé wizard

17. To copy selected text to another location with the mouse:

    a. Drag-and-drop the selected text

    b. Double-click the desired location

    c. Print the document and photocopy it

    d. Drag-and-drop the selected text while pressing [Ctrl]

18. A template differs from a wizard in that:

    a. A template contains no graphic items

    b. A wizard creates the document for you based on answers you give

    c. Documents created with a template cannot be changed

    d. A wizard doesn't allow you to enter information

19. To select the text from the insertion point to the end of the line:

    a. Click the paragraph mark

    b. Press [Ctrl]+[Home]

    c. Click in the selection bar

    d. Press [Shift]+[End]

20. Double-clicking in the selection bar:

    a. Opens the New dialog box

    b. Selects the entire document

    c. Selects the adjacent paragraph

    d. Minimizes the document window

21. The [icon] button:

    a. Inserts the contents of the Clipboard at the insertion point

    b. Copies selected text to the clipboard

    c. Opens a note pane

    d. Views the contents of the Clipboard

Interactivity

Test Your Skills

1. Find a file and open it:

   a. Go to the Open dialog box.

   b. Using the Find section of the Open dialog box, find the student file **SkillTest2**.

   c. Open the file and save it to your student disk as Test 2.

2. Select portions of the document and delete them:

   a. Select the last sentence in the second paragraph, the one that begins, "He was really great...," by clicking it while pressing [Ctrl].

   b. Delete the selected sentence.

   c. Select the postscript at the end of the document by triple-clicking it.

   d. Add the text that extends from the selected paragraph to the end of the document to the selection by pressing [Ctrl]+[Shift]+[End].

   e. Delete the selection.

3. Select paragraphs in the document and move them:

   a. Select the third paragraph, the one that begins, "On a slightly different note...," by double-clicking next to it in the selection bar.

   b. Drag the selected paragraph to the blank line following the next paragraph and drop it there.

   c. Select the first paragraph by triple-clicking it.

   d. Cut the selected paragraph and send it to the Clipboard by using the Cut command.

   e. Paste the copy at the end of the final paragraph of the document, before the signature.

4. Use Word's Help facility to find out about Microsoft FastTips:

   a. Open the Help Topics window by clicking Help, then clicking Contents and Index.

   b. On the Index tab, type help and press [Enter].

   c. Double-click on FastTips.

   d. When you are finished learning about FastTips, close the Help windows.

   e. Close the document, saving changes if prompted.

Interactivity (continued)

Problem Solving

Using the skills you learned in Lesson 2, use the Résumé Wizard to create a Professional, Entry-level résumé to accompany the letter you wrote at the end of Lesson 1. Be sure to include your current address, career objectives, education, job experience, other relevant experience, interests and activities. When the wizard has created the résumé, use the Cut and Paste commands and the drag-and-drop method to rearrange the order of the résumé sections. Then print out a copy of the finished résumé and save the file to your student disk as **Solved2**.

L E S S O N

3

FORMATTING

Word allows you to add many different types of formatting to a document. These can be broken down into three major divisions: text-level formatting, paragraph-level formatting, and document-level formatting.

Text-level formatting, which was covered in Lesson 1, refers to all formatting that applies to individual characters in a document, such as size, font, and such options as bold and italics. No matter where text appears, these characteristics can be applied to single letters or entire sections of text.

Paragraph-level formatting covers the characteristics that can be applied to a paragraph or group of paragraphs. These include alignment, indents, line spacing, line numbers, and other aspects that cannot be applied to a single character.

Document-level formatting includes such options as margins and headers and footers, which are items set to appear on every page of a document, including page numbers and the document title.

Once the document has been completed and formatted to meet your needs, Word offers several proofreading aids to assure the quality of the finished product. In addition to a spelling checker that spots misspelled words throughout the document, Word has a feature called AutoCorrect that can actually fix common typing and spelling mistakes automatically, as they are made. Word also contains a built-in thesaurus that makes finding the perfect word both simple and fast. And if you decide to change a word or phrase that occurs in several places in a long document, Word can search your document for all instances of the item and replace them with something you prefer.

Case Study:
In this lesson, Sabrina will add formatting to a research paper that she has written and will add data that has been collected by her research partner, Juan. She and Juan will then proofread the document and make corrections.

 # Formatting a Document

Concept

Word provides control over many aspects of formatting at the document level. These include margins, paper size, and layout.

Do It!

Sabrina wants to reduce the left and right margins of a research paper she has been working on.

1 Open the student file **Doit3-1** and save it to your student disk as **Report.doc**.

2 Click **File**, then click **Page Setup**. The Page Setup dialog box appears.

3 Click the **Margins** tab to bring it to the front if it is not already foremost in the dialog box, as shown in Figure 3-1.

4 Click the downward-pointing arrow on the side of the **Left** box three times to reduce the Word default setting from 1.25 inches to 1 inch. The Preview box reflects the change you made to the left margin.

5 Triple-click the **Right** box to select it.

6 Type the number 1 to replace the selected value of 1.25. Since inches is the default setting for measurement, you do not need to enter its symbol.

7 Click [OK] to apply the changes to the document and close the dialog box. The text of your document may now extend beyond the edge of your screen. You can adjust this by reducing the zoom factor on the Standard toolbar. Do not close the document, as you will be using the same one throughout the next several Skills.

More

The **Margins** tab of the Page Setup dialog box also enables you to adjust the margins at the top and bottom of your pages as well as the left and right margins of headers and footers, which are items at the top or bottom of a page that remain constant across many pages. These can include such things as page numbers, logos, or the title of the document. The **Paper Size** tab lets you format a document to fit any size medium (such as legal-size paper or an envelope) that your printer can handle. The **Paper Source** tab tells the printer where to get the right size paper for your document. The Paper Source and Paper Size tabs will offer different options depending upon the current selected printer. The **Page Layout** tab lets you control the vertical alignment of text on each page and allows you to add line numbers to the document.

Figure 3-1 Margins tab of the Page Setup dialog box

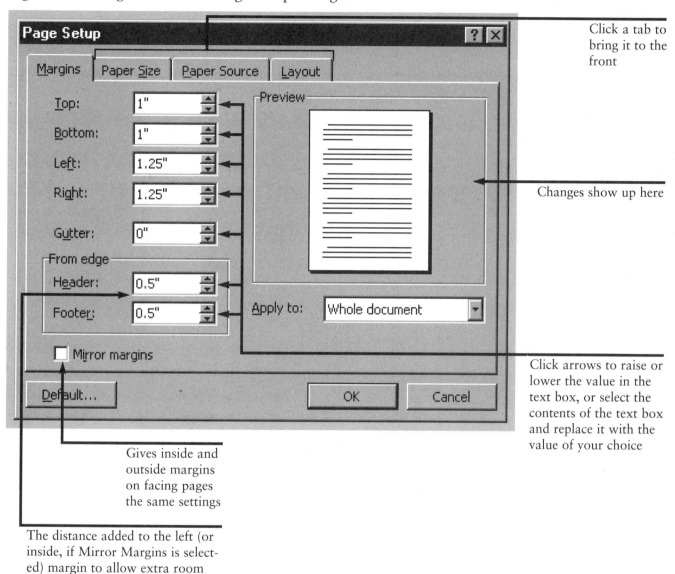

Click a tab to bring it to the front

Changes show up here

Click arrows to raise or lower the value in the text box, or select the contents of the text box and replace it with the value of your choice

Gives inside and outside margins on facing pages the same settings

The distance added to the left (or inside, if Mirror Margins is selected) margin to allow extra room for binding

Practice

To practice adjusting margins in a document, open the student file **Prac3-1**.

Hot Tip

You can put different kinds of document formatting, such as margins, in one document by changing the setting of the **Apply To** box on the Layout tab of the Page Setup dialog box from Whole Document to This Point Forward.

 **Inserting
Page Numbers**

Concept

Word can insert **page numbers** into documents in a variety of placement locations and styles.

Do It!

Sabrina wants to add centered page numbers to the report and view them.

1 Click **Insert**, then click **Page Numbers** to bring up its dialog box, as shown in Figure 3-2.

2 Click the **Alignment** box, then click **Center** to change the horizontal position of each page number from the default right setting to center.

3 Click [Format...] to bring up the Page Number Format dialog box.

4 Make sure the **Number Format** box displays Arabic numerals (1, 2, 3...) instead of letters or Roman numerals. If it does not, click the box, then click **1,2,3...** to select Arabic numerals.

5 Click [OK] to leave the Format dialog box and return to the Page Numbers dialog box.

6 Click [OK] to confirm and apply the page numbering. Word automatically shifts to Page Layout View so that the page numbers can be seen.

7 Scroll to the bottom of the page to see the inserted page number.

More

The numbers you have added to the document do not appear in **Normal View**. As you may recall, however, Word allows you to view your document in different ways. For example, the Print Preview screen offers a quick way to see how your document will look when printed, without nonprinting characters but including items not seen in the default Normal View, such as headers, footers, and page numbers. With the View menu, Word offers other ways of looking at your document. The **Outline View** is helpful when you use Word's outlining features to structure your text with headings and subheadings. **Online Layout View** includes a document map that makes moving from location to location in a document easier. Like Print Preview, **Page Layout View** allows you to see your document as it will appear when printed, including page numbers, but retains the Ruler and the Standard and Formatting toolbars and lacks the Print Preview toolbar and magnifying tool. You can quickly move between these different views by using the **View** buttons at the left end of the horizontal scroll bar at the bottom of the window. The current view is indicated by its depressed button next to the horizontal scroll bar and on the View menu. Other view options include **Header and Footer** and **Full Screen**, which shows only the document. The **Toolbars** submenu on the View menu lets you select which toolbars appear on the screen.

Figure 3-2   Page Numbers dialog box

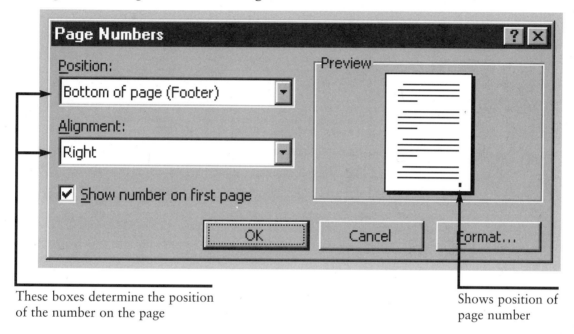

These boxes determine the position
of the number on the page

Shows position of
page number

Practice

To practice inserting page numbers, open
the student file **Prac3-2**.

Hot Tip

The View buttons to the left of the
horizontal scroll bar are not available in
Online Layout View.

Inserting Footnotes and Endnotes

Concept

A **footnote** explains text in a document at the bottom of the page where the text appears. An **endnote** provides an explanation at the end of a document. Both contain two parts: a note reference mark and the note text. Word automates the process of creating and numbering footnotes and endnotes.

Do It!

Sabrina would like to add a footnote to her research paper.

1 Position the insertion point at the end of the first paragraph, after the words "their work done." This is where the note reference mark will appear.

2 Click **Insert**, then click **Footnote**. The Footnote and Endnote dialog box appears with Footnote (the Word default) selected, as shown in Figure 3-3.

3 Click [OK] to insert the footnote using current settings. Word inserts the note reference mark at the insertion point and opens a note pane at the bottom of the window.

4 Type the following text:
These "anytime, anywhere" work environments are sometimes called "virtual offices," because work can be performed outside the traditional physical office setting and work schedule.

5 Click [Close] to leave the note pane and return to the document window.

6 If you are not already in Page Layout View, click **View**, then click **Page Layout View** to get there. Then you can scroll to the bottom of the page and view the footnote in its proper place. Alternately, you can position the mouse pointer over the reference mark; the footnote will appear as a ScreenTip.

More

The note pane is a separate part of the document window where footnote text is entered. All footnotes in each document are accessible through the note pane. In the Footnote dialog box, the **AutoNumber** option is the default setting. With this option selected, Word will automatically renumber the note reference marks if you add or remove some of your footnotes or endnotes, so there will be no break in their continuity. The default formatting for footnote text is 10 point Times New Roman, aligned left. This can be changed just as you would change the formatting of any other text in a document. The **Note Options** dialog box, accessed by clicking [Options...] in the Footnote and Endnote dialog box, offers further flexibility in number format and note placement.

Like page numbers, footnotes and endnotes do not appear as part of the document in the Normal View. You can view and edit a footnote by double-clicking its reference mark in the text, which opens the note pane. Switching to Page Layout View shows the footnotes below a horizontal line at the bottom of a page or endnotes at the end of the document as they will appear on the actual page.

Figure 3-3   Footnote and Endnote dialog box

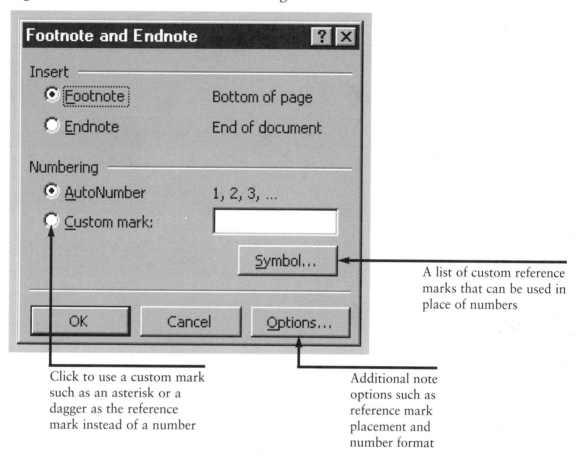

A list of custom reference marks that can be used in place of numbers

Click to use a custom mark such as an asterisk or a dagger as the reference mark instead of a number

Additional note options such as reference mark placement and number format

Practice

To practice inserting Footnotes into a document, open the student file **Prac3-3**.

Hot Tip

When a note pane is open, you can go to the next pane by pressing **[F6]** or to the previous pane by pressing **[Shift]+[F6]**.

INTERACTIVE   COMPUTING   •   Word

Skill Applying Indents

Concept

Paragraph indents may be changed easily using the four indent markers on the ruler, or the Paragraph formatting dialog box may be used for more precise control.

Do It!

Sabrina wants to indent the first line of each paragraph in the main text by half an inch and apply a hanging indent to her References section.

1 Select the four paragraphs of main text by clicking before the first word of the first paragraph, scrolling down to the end of the document and holding [Shift] while clicking after the last word of the fourth paragraph. The entire document should be selected between the heading and References sections.

2 Click and drag the **First line indent marker** in the ruler (see Figure 3-4) to the half-inch mark. The first line of each paragraph will move to the right half an inch.

3 Deselect the main text by clicking once anywhere in the document window.

4 Select the entire References section of Sabrina's report, from the word "References" to the end of the document.

5 Click and drag the **Hanging indent marker** in the ruler to the half-inch mark. (The Left indent marker will move with it.) All lines in a paragraph that are not first lines move to the right half an inch. This is called a **hanging indent** because it leaves the first line hanging at the left margin.

More

All markers on the ruler may be changed by clicking and dragging. The First line indent marker, as seen above, controls the indentation of the first line of selected paragraphs. The Hanging indent marker determines the amount of indentation from the left margin of all lines of a selected paragraph except its first line. The rectangle below the Hanging indent marker is called the Left indent marker and determines the amount of indentation for all lines of a selected paragraph, including the first line. Finally, the Right indent marker at the right end of the ruler regulates the amount of indentation from the right margin for all lines of a selected paragraph. The default settings for all of the indent markers are even with the margins.

You can also indent the first line of paragraphs as you type with the **Tab** key. Each time you press [Tab], the insertion point jumps to the next **tab stop**. Word's default tab settings are one-half inch. You can also set your own tab stops by clicking the bottom half of the ruler where you want them. After they are set, tab stops can be moved by dragging them along the ruler with the mouse pointer. To remove a tab stop, click the one you wish to remove and drag it below the ruler. It will vanish when the mouse button is released. Clicking the tab alignment selector at the left end of the ruler selects different tab alignments that can be applied. Table 3-1 describes the various tab alignments and their properties.

The tab and indent settings can also be adjusted from the **Paragraph** dialog box on the **Format** menu, as shown in Figure 3-5. Any indent changes made with the ruler will show up in the indent settings of the dialog box and vice versa.

Figure 3-4 Horizontal ruler

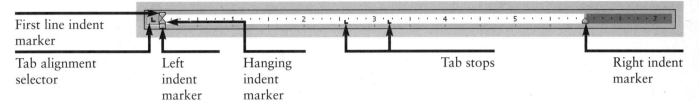

First line indent
marker

Tab alignment
selector

Left
indent
marker

Hanging
indent
marker

Tab stops

Right indent
marker

Table 3-1   Alignment of Various Tabs

Tab Alignment	Properties	Button
Left	Text extends from the tab stop to the right	L
Center	Text is centered on the tab stop	⊥
Right	Text extends from the tab stop to the left	⌐
Decimal	The decimal point in the text aligns itself beneath the tab stop; text before the decimal is to the left of the tab stop, text after it is to the right	⊥

Figure 3-5 Adjusting indents from the Paragraph dialog box

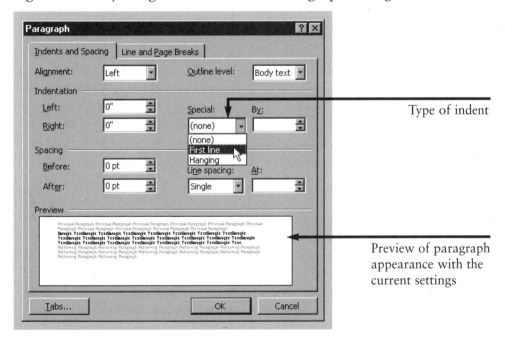

Type of indent

Preview of paragraph
appearance with the
current settings

 # Changing Line Spacing

Concept

The **line spacing**, or distance between adjacent horizontal lines of text, can be modified from the **Paragraph** dialog box. Word also allows the user to change the spacing between paragraphs.

Do It!

Sabrina wants to remove the spaces between paragraphs and double-space her report.

1. Delete each of the blank lines between the four paragraphs of the main text by selecting the blank lines and pressing [**Delete**].

2. Click **Edit**, then click **Select All** to select the entire document.

3. Click **Format**, then click **Paragraph** to bring up the Paragraph dialog box.

4. Click the **Line Spacing** list box, then click **Double**. (See Figure 3-6.)

5. Click   OK   to accept the changes you have made. All paragraphs in the document are now double-spaced.

More

The Paragraph formatting dialog box has a **Preview** box that allows you to see how the changes you are making will affect your text. The Word default setting is single spacing. If the spacing interval you want is not available in the Line Spacing list box, the **At** box allows you to set your spacing at any interval you enter, such as 1.25 or 0.9. The **Before** and **After** boxes refer to the spacing before and after each selected paragraph. This allows you to automatically space paragraphs at any interval without adding blank lines to the document.

Figure 3-6 Adjusting line spacing from the Paragraph dialog box

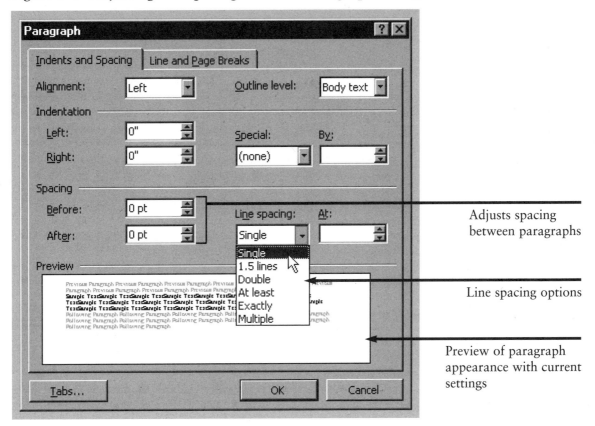

<table>
<tr><td></td><td>Adjusts spacing
between paragraphs</td></tr>
<tr><td></td><td>Line spacing options</td></tr>
<tr><td></td><td>Preview of paragraph
appearance with current
settings</td></tr>
</table>

Practice

To practice changing line spacing and paragraph spacing, open the student file **Prac3-5**.

Hot Tip

When formatting the paragraphs in a document, it is often helpful to show nonprinting characters with the  button.

Inserting
Page Breaks

Concept

The dotted horizontal line that divides pages in a document in the Normal View (or the clear separation between pages in Page Layout View) is called a **soft page break**. It will shift position as lines are added or removed from a document. Likewise, when enough text has been entered to fill a page, Word will create another page. A **hard page break**, also known as a **manual page break**, can be inserted where a page break will always occur, regardless of deletions or additions to previous text.

Do It!

Sabrina wants to put the References section of her report on a separate page.

1. Place the insertion point before the word "References" at the head of the References section of the report. This will become the first line of the new References page.

2. Click **Insert,** then click **Break.** The Break dialog box appears with Page Break preselected, as shown in Figure 3-7.

3. Click [OK] to insert a page break at the insertion point. The References section will now appear at the top of a new page. Word will automatically renumber the pages of the document to account for the new page.

More

A hard page break looks the same as a soft page break, except the words "Page Break" appear in the center of the solid horizontal line dividing the page. You can remove a hard page break by clicking next to it in the selection bar to select it and then pressing [Delete]. The Break dialog box also allows you to add **section breaks.** A **section** is just a distinct part of your document that is separated from the rest. For example, chapters in a book can be manipulated as sections. Inserting a section break ends a section and dictates where the next will begin. When you choose the **Next Page** section break option from the Break dialog box, Word breaks the page at the section break and the next section begins at the top of the next page. When you click **Continuous,** Word inserts a section break and starts a new section on the same page. Clicking **Odd Page** or **Even Page** begins the new section on the next odd-numbered page or the next even-numbered page. (See Figure 3-8.)

Figure 3-7 Break dialog box

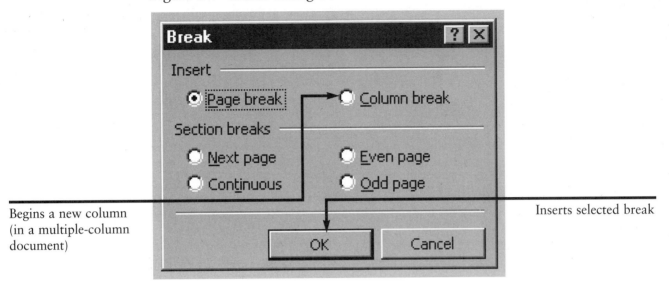

Begins a new column
(in a multiple-column
document)

Inserts selected break

Figure 3-8 Types of section breaks

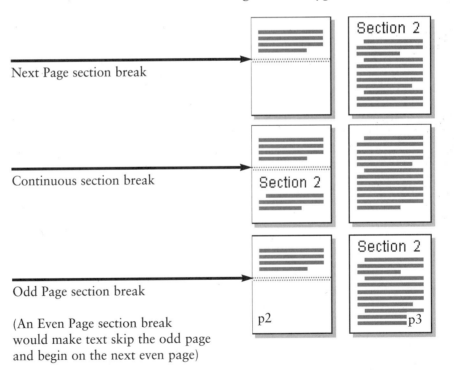

Next Page section break

Continuous section break

Odd Page section break

(An Even Page section break
would make text skip the odd page
and begin on the next even page)

 **Working with Multiple Documents**

Concept

Word, like many other Windows programs, lets the user **work with more than one document at a time**. A new document can be created or an existing one opened without jeopardizing the currently active document. Document windows can be arranged so that one, two, or all open documents may be seen simultaneously. In addition, text can be copied and moved between open documents by using the Clipboard.

Do It!

Sabrina wants to combine text that she and her partner, Juan, have written.

1. Open the student file **Doit3-7**. This is Juan's contribution to their report. Sabrina's portion (Report.doc) will remain open but will be hidden behind the newly opened document.

2. Click **Edit**, then click **Select All** to select Juan's document.

3. Click the **Copy** button on the Standard toolbar to copy Juan's document to the Clipboard.

4. Click **Window**, then click **Report.doc** to bring Sabrina's report to the front. The Window menu shows all open Word documents, with a check next to the active document.

5. Place the insertion point just before the second paragraph in her report, the one that begins, "There are both…."

6. Click the **Paste** button to insert Juan's text into their report. Notice that his text conforms to the document-wide settings that Sabrina set earlier. Its margins change from 1.25 to 1 inch to match the rest of the document. It remains single-spaced, however, as line spacing is formatted at the paragraph level. The text will be cleaned up in the next Skill.

More

There are several ways to move between various open Word documents. The Window menu shows all open Word documents, and on the File menu there is a list of documents that Word has worked with recently. The number of recently opened documents displayed here can be altered from the General tab in the Options dialog box found on the Tools menu. There is also a list of recently opened files on the Documents menu available on the Windows Start menu. Clicking one of these will open it, or bring it to the front if it is already open. The Clipboard can be used to transfer data between documents in the same way it is used within a single document. The active window is always the one in front. If the active window is not maximized, you may be able to see inactive windows behind it. (See Figure 3-9.)

Figure 3-9 Activating inactive document windows

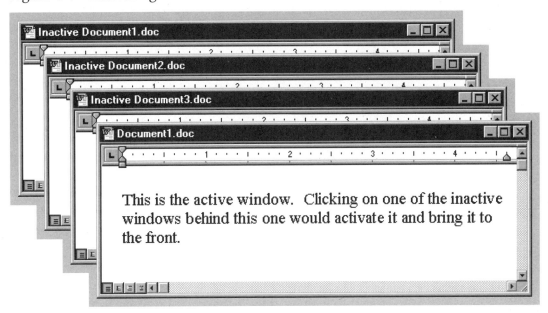

Practice

To practice moving text between two documents, open the student file **Prac3-7**.

Hot Tip

You can move a window that is not maximized by clicking in its title bar and dragging it.

Skill

Using the Format Painter

Concept

The **Format Painter** makes it possible to copy the formatting settings from selected text to another section of text.

Do It!

Sabrina would like to format Juan's text like the rest of her document.

1 Select Sabrina's first paragraph by double-clicking next to it in the selection bar.

2 Click the **Format Painter** button on the Standard toolbar. The mouse pointer will appear as an I-beam with a paintbrush next to it as it moves over areas that have formatting differing from that of the selected text. This indicates that the formatting of the selected text has been copied and is ready to be applied to a new area. (See Figure 3-10.)

3 Click Juan's paragraph (not his references) to automatically format it to match Sabrina's text.

4 Select the three lines of Juan's references by clicking next to the first line in the selection bar and dragging down to select the other two lines as well.

5 Click and drag the selected text to the very end of the document, releasing the mouse button after moving the dotted insertion point to the right of Sabrina's last reference. Now all references are in their proper place in the References section.

6 Select one of Sabrina's references by double-clicking next to it in the selection bar.

7 Click the **Format Painter** button to copy her formatting settings.

8 Select the three lines of Juan's references by clicking next to the first line in the selection bar and dragging down to select the other two lines as well. Now all the references follow Sabrina's formatting.

9 Click **Window**, then click **Doit3-7.doc** to go back to Juan's document.

10 Click **File**, then click **Close** to close Juan's document. Do **not** save changes.

11 Click **File**, then **Close** again to close Sabrina's document. This time, save changes when prompted.

More

To format more than one area with the same selected format settings, double-click the Format Painter button. When you have formatted all the text you need, click the button again to turn off the Format Painter. If you only want to copy the character formatting, don't include the paragraph mark ¶ at the end of the text you are formatting. Remember, the paragraph mark is the place in the text where [Enter] was pressed to go to a new line; it can be displayed by clicking the **Show/Hide** ¶ button on the Standard toolbar. If the text you have selected to format includes the paragraph mark, the paragraph formatting will be copied too. The collection of all formatting characteristics of a document is referred to as its style. The **Style Gallery**, available on the Format menu, allows you to apply styles from any of Word's templates to the current document. These styles include the margins, text formatting, indents, and other format options existing in the document style you choose.

Figure 3-10 Copying the formatting of a paragraph with the Format Painter

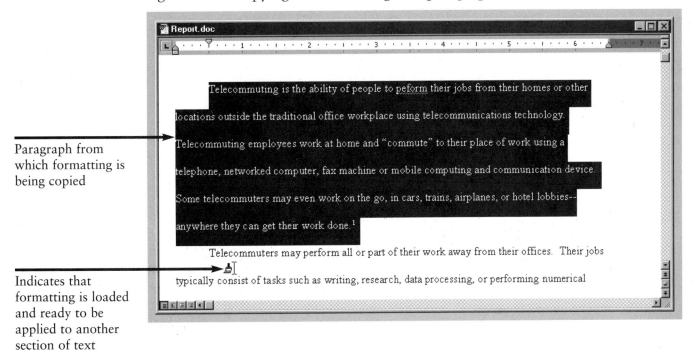

Paragraph from which formatting is being copied

Indicates that formatting is loaded and ready to be applied to another section of text

Practice

To practice using the Format Painter, open the student file **Prac3-8**.

Hot Tip

The Style Gallery dialog box allows you to preview the selected template by itself, or as it would appear applied either to your document or to a sample document.

Checking Spelling and Grammar

Concept

Word has the ability to **check the spelling and grammar** in a document and offer suggestions to correct words that its built-in dictionary does not contain and words and phrases that it believes to be grammatically incorrect.

Do It!

Sabrina wants to check a document for spelling and grammar errors.

1 Open the student file **Doit3-9** and save it to your student disk as **Spelling**. This is a sample paragraph with several spelling and grammar errors in it.

2 Right-click (click with the right mouse button) on the first word in the paragraph that is underlined with a wavy red line, **processer**. A pop-up menu appears with several suggested correct spellings. As shown in Figure 3-11, move the mouse over the list to select the first choice, **processor**, and click. Word replaces the misspelled word with the selected alternative.

3 Click **Tools**, then click **Spelling and Grammar**. The Spelling and Grammar dialog box will appear, as shown in Figure 3-12, with the first error highlighted in red and suggestions for replacing it below.

4 Select the second word in the Suggestions box, **grammar**, and click [Change All] to correct all occurrences of this spelling mistake throughout the document. Word then highlights a repeated word.

5 Click [Delete], which appears in place of the Change button. The second "you" disappears. Word now detects a grammatical error in the document, noting that the verb "provide" does not agree with its subject, "it."

6 Click [Change] to change the highlighted word to "provides," thereby creating agreement between subject and verb and clarifying the meaning of the sentence. The spelling and grammar checker highlights a name, which it does not recognize.

Figure 3-11 Automatic spell checking

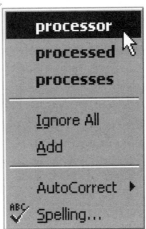

Figure 3-12 Spelling and Grammar dialog box

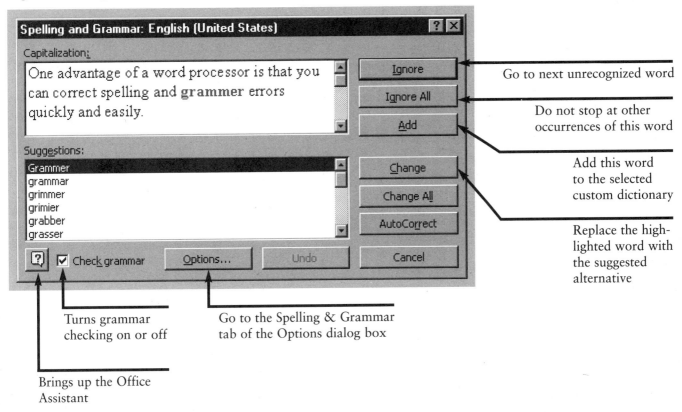

Go to next unrecognized word

Do not stop at other
occurrences of this word

Add this word
to the selected
custom dictionary

Replace the high-
lighted word with
the suggested
alternative

Turns grammar
checking on or off

Go to the Spelling & Grammar
tab of the Options dialog box

Brings up the Office
Assistant

Skill Checking Spelling and Grammar (continued)

Do It!

7 Click [Ignore] to ignore the selected word, which, though Word doesn't recognize it, is spelled correctly. Word now highlights a misspelled word.

8 Click [Change]. Word replaces "simpley" with the correct spelling, "simply," and the Spelling and Grammar dialog box disappears, replaced with a small Microsoft Word message box notifying you that no further errors were found and that the check is complete.

9 Click [OK]. The message box disappears.

10 Save and close the document.

More

In the same way that the Change All button in the Spelling dialog box causes Word to correct all further instances of the selected word, the **Ignore All** button causes Word to skip over all instances of an unrecognized word throughout the document. Word takes capitalization into account when checking spelling, so if it was told to ignore "Microwaveable," for example, it would still stop on "microwaveable" if it were to appear elsewhere in the document. The reason that different copies of Word may recognize different words is that words can be permanently added to Word's **custom dictionary**, a document that is unique to each copy of Microsoft Word. If you should choose to click [Add] in the Spelling and Grammar dialog box when the spell checker highlights a word it does not know but that you know is spelled correctly, the word will be added to the custom dictionary and will not be questioned again. You may freely edit the sentence appearing in the Not in Dictionary box just as you would edit it in your document; changes you make to the sentence will take effect when the spelling and grammar checker goes on to the next error.

Word's **Automatic Spell Check** feature was briefly mentioned in Lesson 1. As you type, Word can underline with a wavy red line words that it does not recognize. Likewise, it underlines with a wavy green line words or phrases that it believes are grammatically incorrect. Right-clicking a word underlined in red in this fashion brings up a pop-up menu that contains a list of suggested alternatives to the underlined word, the Ignore All and Add commands, and a shortcut to the Spelling dialog box. Clicking one of the alternate words on the list will change the underlined word to match it. There is also an AutoCorrect option, which you will learn more about in the next Skill. When a word that is underlined with a green wavy line is right-clicked, a similar pop-up menu appears with a list of suggested alternatives, an Ignore Sentence option, and a shortcut to the Grammar dialog box. The Check spelling as you type and Check grammar as you type options can be turned on or off from the Spelling & Grammar tab of the Options dialog box (Figure 3-13), available on the Tools menu or by clicking [Options...] on the Spelling and Grammar dialog box.

Figure 3-13 Spelling & Grammar tab of the Options dialog box

Turn Automatic Spell
Checking on and off

Customize search

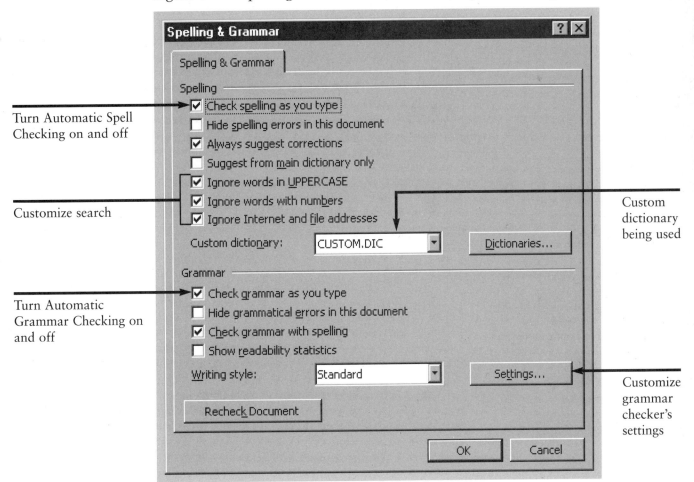

Custom
dictionary
being used

Turn Automatic
Grammar Checking on
and off

Customize
grammar
checker's
settings

Practice

To practice using the spell checker, open
the student file **Prac3-9**.

Hot Tip

You can create more than one custom
dictionary, but Word comes equipped with
only one.

Using AutoCorrect

Concept

Word's **AutoCorrect** feature corrects specified mistakes automatically as they are entered and can be modified to accommodate a wide variety of errors. For example, it can automatically capitalize the first letter of a sentence.

Do It!

Sabrina wants to set AutoCorrect to automatically fix a typing mistake she often makes.

1 Open a new blank document by clicking the **New** button on the Standard tool-bar.

2 Click **Tools**, then **AutoCorrect**. The AutoCorrect dialog box appears with the insertion point in the **Replace** box, as shown in Figure 3-14.

3 Type the word **corect** in the Replace box. (It is misspelled here intentionally.)

4 Press [**Tab**] to move the insertion point to the **With** box.

5 Type the word **correct**. Word will now replace "corect" with "correct" in any document.

6 Click ▢ OK ▢ to accept the changes you have made and to leave the AutoCorrect dialog box. The blank document that you created in the first step is now in the active window.

7 Type the following sentence exactly as it appears: **Word will now corect mistakes i make.** Notice that as you typed the sentence, Word automatically fixed the misspelled "corect" and capitalized the letter "i."

Figure 3-14 AutoCorrect dialog box

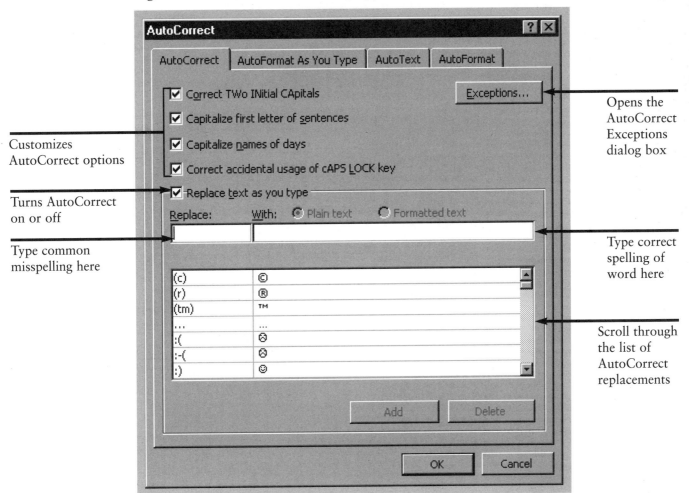

Customizes
AutoCorrect options

Turns AutoCorrect
on or off

Type common
misspelling here

Opens the
AutoCorrect
Exceptions
dialog box

Type correct
spelling of
word here

Scroll through
the list of
AutoCorrect
replacements

67

Using AutoCorrect

(continued)

Do It!

⑧ Press [Space] after the previous sentence, then type the word **many** (lowercase, as shown) followed by a space. Word recognizes "many" to be the first word of a new sentence because it is preceded by a period and a space, and therefore capitalizes it.

⑨ Type **misc. mistakes are fixed automatically.** Notice that although you typed a period and a space after "misc," the word "mistakes" was not capitalized. This is because "misc." is on Word's AutoCorrect Exceptions list along with most other common abbreviations.

⑩ Close the document. Do not save changes.

More

Word's AutoCorrect Exceptions dialog box, shown in Figure 3-15, can be accessed by clicking `Exceptions...` in the AutoCorrect dialog box. Word will recognize the period and space after one of the abbreviations on this list as differing from those at the end of a sentence, and will not capitalize the next word. To get rid of an AutoCorrect entry that you don't want, select the entry in the AutoCorrect dialog box and click `Delete`.

While AutoCorrect fixes spelling errors in words you have finished typing, Word's AutoComplete feature recognizes many words and phrases as you are typing them, predicts the outcome, and offers to complete them for you. For example, if you type "Dear M," Word will suggest "Dear Mom and Dad." If Word recognizes that what you are typing matches a word or phrase contained in its list of AutoText entries, a ScreenTip will appear with Word's guess as to what you wish to type. If the suggestion is correct, press the enter key to insert the finished text. If not, simply continue typing and the ScreenTip will disappear. Use the AutoText tab of the AutoCorrect dialog box (shown in Figure 3-16) to add to the list of terms that AutoComplete will recognize. You can also see what AutoText entries are available by clicking `All Entries ▾` on the AutoText toolbar. Clicking one of the AutoText entries inserts it into your document at the insertion point. Some AutoText entries automatically include relevant data. If the insertion point is on the fourth page of a ten-page document and you insert the AutoText entry "Page X of Y," for instance, Word will insert "Page 4 of 10."

Figure 3-15 AutoCorrect Exceptions dialog box

Type new abbreviation here to
include it on the exceptions list

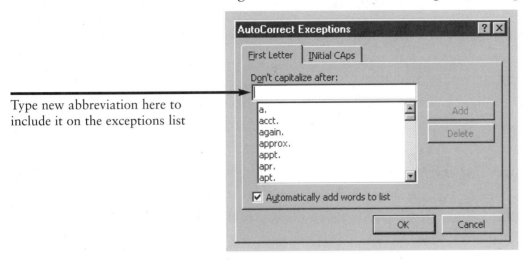

Figure 3-16 AutoText tab of the AutoCorrect dialog box

Turns
AutoComplete
on or off

Brings up the
AutoText toolbar

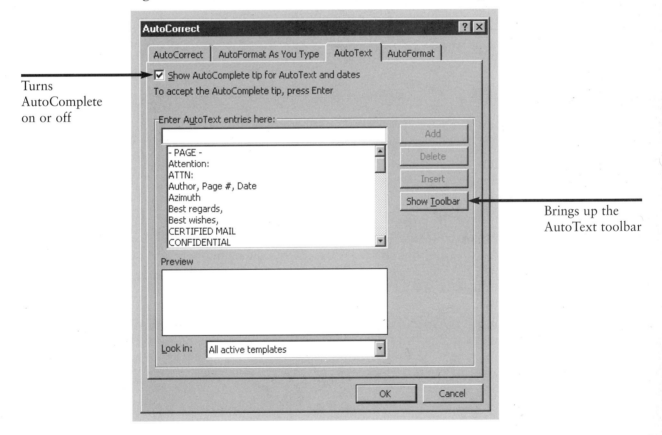

Practice

To practice using Word's AutoCorrect feature, open the student file **Prac3-10**.

Hot Tip

When the **Automatically Add Words to
List** check box on the AutoCorrect
Exceptions dialog box is checked, words
may be added to the list by pressing
[Backspace] and typing over the correction.

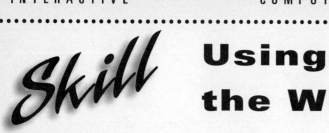
Using the Word Thesaurus

Concept

Word contains a **Thesaurus** facility that can suggest synonyms and antonyms for words that you select.

Do It!

Sabrina wants to find a more descriptive word than the one she used in one of her sentences.

1. Open the student file **Doit3-11** and save it as **Report2.doc**. It is a copy of Sabrina and Juan's report that has been fully spell checked.

2. Select the word **hard** in the fifth sentence of the third paragraph of the report, the sentence that begins, "Many telecommuters are not locked into a hard 9-to-5 work schedule...."

3. Click **Tools**, then click **Thesaurus** on the **Language** submenu. The Thesaurus dialog box appears with the word "hard" displayed in the **Looked Up** box, as shown in Figure 3-17.

4. Click the word **inflexible** in the **Replace with Synonym** box to select it.

5. Click [Look Up] to search for synonyms of "inflexible."

6. Click the word **rigid** in the Replace with Synonym box to select it.

7. Click [Replace] to insert "rigid" in place of "hard" in the report.

More

The **Meanings** box in the Thesaurus dialog box shows the various possible meanings of the selected word. Depending on the word, the Meanings box may also have Antonym or Related Words listed, which will show you opposite meanings and words with similar structure, respectively.

Word can also quickly count and display the number of pages, words, characters, paragraphs, and lines in your document. To bring up the **Word Count** dialog box (shown in Figure 3-18) with all the information already calculated for the open document, simply click **Tools**, then click **Word Count**.

Figure 3-17 Thesaurus dialog box

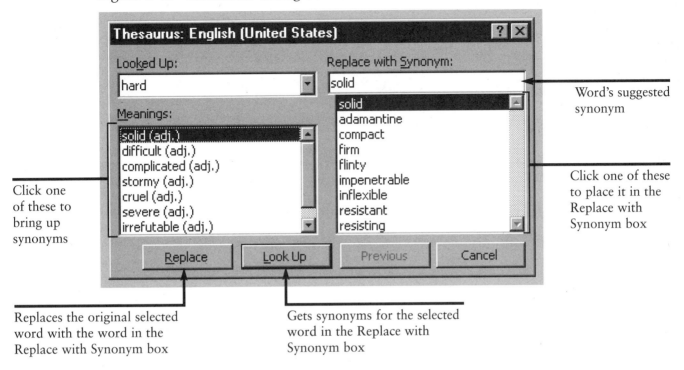

Click one
of these to
bring up
synonyms

Word's suggested
synonym

Click one of these
to place it in the
Replace with
Synonym box

Replaces the original selected
word with the word in the
Replace with Synonym box

Gets synonyms for the selected
word in the Replace with
Synonym box

Figure 3-18 Word Count dialog box

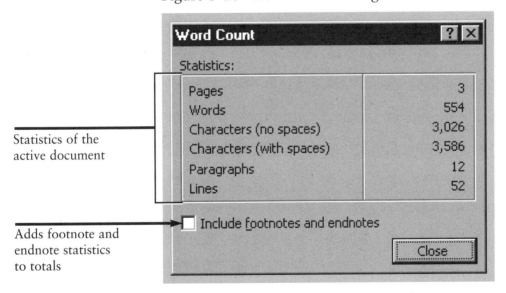

Statistics of the
active document

Adds footnote and
endnote statistics
to totals

Practice

To practice using the Thesaurus, open the student file **Prac3-11**.

Hot Tip

Click the **Looked Up** drop-down list arrow on the Thesaurus dialog box to view all words that have been looked up during the current search, with the original selected word at the bottom.

Finding
and Replacing Text

Concept

The **Find** and **Replace** commands allow a document to be searched for individual occurrences of any word, phrase, or other unit of text that can then be replaced by a preferred item.

Do It!

Sabrina and Juan have used both "per cent" and "percent" in their report and, though both spellings are correct, they want to spell the word consistently throughout their document.

1 Place the insertion point at the beginning of the document. Word will search the document from the insertion point forward.

2 Click **Edit**, then click **Replace**. The Find and Replace dialog box appears with the Replace tab in front and the insertion point in the **Find What** text box, as shown in Figure 3-19.

3 Type **per cent** into the Find What text box.

4 Click the **Replace With** text box to move the insertion point there.

5 Type **percent** as one word in the Replace With text box.

6 Click [Replace All] to search the document for all instances of "per cent" and replace them with "percent." A message box appears to display the results. In this case, one replacement was made.

7 Click [OK] to close the message box.

8 Close the Find and Replace dialog box.

9 Save and close the document.

More

You can examine and replace each instance of a word individually instead of automatically by clicking the **Find Next** button instead of **Replace All**. The **Search** drop-down list determines the direction of the search relative to the insertion point; you can search upward or downward through the document or keep the Word default setting of **All**, which checks the entire document including headers, footers, and footnotes. The five check boxes control other Find options, as explained in Table 3-2. The **Format** drop-down list contains formatting specifications, such as bold text or a particular indent depth, that Word can search for and replace. The **Special** drop-down list shows special characters that Word can search for, such as paragraph marks, manual page breaks or a particular letter or digit. The **No Formatting** button removes all formatting criteria from your search parameters.

The **Find** tab of the Find and Replace dialog box is identical to the Replace tab except it lacks the replace function and merely searches your document for the items you specify.

Figure 3-19 Find and Replace dialog box

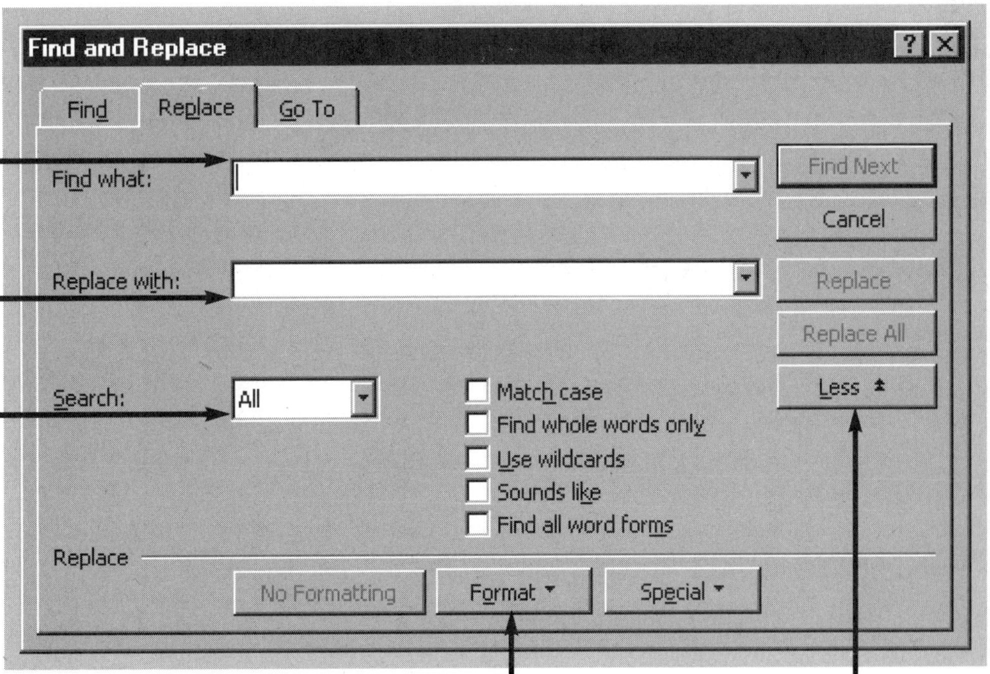

Enter the word you
want to search for and
replace here

Enter the replacement
word here

Defines search direction

Find and Replace

Find | Replace | Go To

Find what:

Replace with:

Search: All

Find Next
Cancel
Replace
Replace All
Less ±

☐ Match case
☐ Find whole words only
☐ Use wildcards
☐ Sounds like
☐ Find all word forms

Replace

No Formatting | Format ▼ | Special ▼

A submenu of dialog boxes
that enable you to search for
very specific formatting items

Shrinks dialog box to
show fewer options

Table 3-2   Find Options

Option	Description
Match case	Finds only text with uppercase and lowercase letters that match exactly the contents of the Find What text box
Find whole words only	Disregards larger words that contain the word that is being searched for
Use wildcards	Searches for wildcards, special characters, or special search operators that are in the Find What box. These can be added from the Special ▼ menu.
Sounds like	Looks for words that sound like the text in the Find What text box but are spelled differently
Find all word forms	Locates all verb forms of a word, such as Do, Doing, Does, and Did

Practice

To practice finding and replacing text, open the student file **Prac3-12**.

Hot Tip

The **Go To** tab on the Find and Replace dialog box is a quick way to get to a particular place in a long document such as a specific page, footnote, or section.

Shortcuts

Function	Button/Mouse	Menu	Keyboard
Adjust margins		Click File, then click Page Setup, then click the Margins tab	
Indent selected paragraphs	Click and drag indent markers on the horizontal ruler	Click Format, then click Paragraph, then click the Indents and Spacing tab	[Ctrl]+[M] (Normal) [Ctrl]+[T] (Hanging)
Adjust Line Spacing of selected paragraphs		Click Format, then click Paragraph, then click the Indents and Spacing tab	[Ctrl]+[1] (Single) [Ctrl]+[2] (Double) [Ctrl]+[5] (1.5)
Go to the next window (When working with multiple documents)	Click on the part of the next window that is showing, if the active window is not maximized	Click Window, then click the name of the next document	[Ctrl]+[F6]
Go to the previous window (When working with multiple documents)	Click on the part of the previous window that is showing, if the active window is not maximized	Click Window, then click the name of the previous document	[Ctrl]+[Shift]+[F6]
Check for spelling and grammar errors		Click Tools, then click Spelling	[F7]
Find next misspelling (With Automatic Spell Checking active)	Scroll down in the document to the next word with a wavy red underline		[Alt]+[F7]
Open the Word Thesaurus		Click Tools, then click Language, then Thesaurus	[Shift]+[F7]

Identify Key Features

Figure 3-20 Identifying formatting concepts

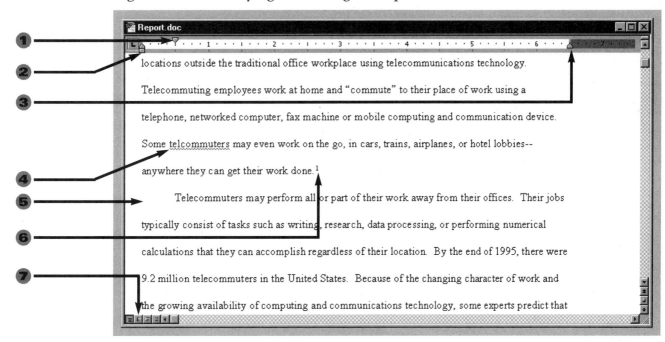

Select the Best Answer

8. Objects that slide along the horizontal ruler and determine text placement

9. A Word feature that fixes common mistakes as they are entered

10. A document where Word places words you "teach" it

11. A line where a new page always begins, regardless of how much space is left on the previous page

12. The place where footnote and endnote text resides

13. The invisible line that marks the boundary between text and the edge of a page

a. Hard Page Break

b. Note Pane

c. AutoCorrect

d. Indent markers

e. Margin

f. Custom dictionary

Quiz (continued)

Complete the Statement

14. Document-level formatting includes:

    a. Indents

    b. Font

    c. Margins

    d. Footnotes

15. A reference mark is:

    a. A mark in the text referring to a footnote or end-note

    b. Another name for a tab stop

    c. Text that has been highlighted

    d. An encyclopedia buyer

16. When there is no more room on a page and more text is entered, Word automatically creates a:

    a. New document based on the Normal template

    b. Manual Page Break

    c. Drop-down list

    d. Soft Page Break

17. AutoCorrect will fix a spelling mistake it recognizes as soon as:

    a. The space bar is pressed

    b. The document is saved

    c. Automatic Spell Checking is turned on

    d. The word matches the first five letters of a spelling mistake on AutoCorrect's list of entries

18. Paragraph-level formatting includes:

    a. Page numbers

    b. Headers and footers

    c. Italics

    d. Line spacing

19. The ⬚ button:

    a. Adds color to text

    b. Copies formatting from one area to another

    c. Pastes the contents of the Clipboard into the document at the insertion point

    d. Displays or hides the Drawing toolbar

20. To copy text from one document to another, you have to:

    a. Set up File Sharing on the Control Panel

    b. Click while pressing [F11]

    c. Use the Clipboard

    d. Use the Style Gallery

Interactivity

Test Your Skills

1. Open a document and format it:

   a. Open the student file **SkillTest 3** and save it to your student disk as **Test 3**.

   b. Open the Page Setup dialog box on the File menu.

   c. Set the left and right margins at 1 inch.

   d. Insert page numbers at the bottom center of the page.

2. Apply indents to the document, change the line spacing, and insert a footnote:

   a. Select all the text of the document below the title.

   b. From the Paragraph dialog box on the Format menu, apply a first line indent of half an inch and change the line spacing to double.

   c. Insert a footnote after the "(p 43)" in the fifth line of the second paragraph of the document reading, "All quotes refer to the revised 1862 edition of the book."

3. Adjust the alignment and text formatting of the document.

   a. Select all the text of the document below the title and justify it.

   b. Select the title and center it.

   c. Boldface the title and the author's name.

4. Open another document and copy text into the original document:

   a. Open the student file **SkillTest 3a** and select the paragraph it contains. It is the conclusion to the paper.

   b. Copy the selected paragraph to the Clipboard.

   c. Close SkillTest 3a, bringing **Test 3** back into the active window.

   d. Place the insertion point at the very end of the document.

   e. Paste the copied paragraph onto the end of the paper.

5. Use the Format Painter to change the formatting of the inserted paragraph to match the rest of the document.

   a. Select the second-to-last paragraph in the document by triple-clicking it.

   b. Click the Format Painter button to copy the formatting of the selected paragraph.

   c. Drag the I-beam (which now has a paintbrush next to it) across the last paragraph in the document to select it and change its formatting to match that of the previous paragraph.

   d. Click once in the paragraph to deselect it.

Interactivity (continued)

Test Your Skills

6. Check for spelling errors and replace all instances of one word with another:

   a. Click Tools, then click Spelling and Grammar to run the Spelling and Grammar Checker. Clear the check grammar check box to check only for spelling errors.

   b. Correct the three misspelled words in the document, ignoring names and unusual words.

   c. Click Edit, then click Replace to open the Replace dialog box.

   d. Use the Replace All command to replace all occurrences of **Browne** with the correct name, **Brown**.

   e. Close the document, saving changes if prompted.

Problem Solving

Using the skills you learned in Lesson 3, open the student file **Problem Solving 3** and save it as **Solved 3**. Change the left and right margins to 1.25", apply a hanging indent of .5" to the document, and change the spacing to 1.5. Add page numbers to the upper left corner of each page, starting on page 1. Center and boldface the title, and justify the main body text of the document. Insert three footnotes into the paper. The text of the footnotes is contained in the student file **Problem Solving 3a**. Insert the first footnote at the end of the third paragraph, following the word "products." The second footnote follows the word "inventory" at the end of the fourth paragraph. The final footnote should be placed after the word "line" at the end of the sixth paragraph. Open the Spell checker and correct all misspellings in the document. Finally, save and close the file.

L E S S O N

4

TABLES AND CHARTS

To more accurately present information in a document, it is often helpful to organize data into a table. Word makes it easy to create and modify tables in its documents, and it has the ability to perform many more complex tasks with data, such as sorting and calculating, that are usually found only in complicated spreadsheet programs.

Word can create blank tables in which data may be entered, or can transform existing data directly into table form. Once a table has been made, data can be quickly inserted or deleted to meet your needs, or reorganized to more effectively get your point across.

Sometimes, it may be difficult to accurately glean trends or important facts from a table, with so much information in text and number form. A chart can be very helpful by presenting the data as a picture that can be more easily grasped and understood.

Case Study:
Juan has accumulated some data for the report that he and Sabrina are working on, and he would like to organize it as a table that will be inserted into the document. Once the table has been finished, he will create a chart based on it and add the chart to the report.

Creating Tables

Concept

A **table** consists of information organized into horizontal **rows** and vertical **columns**. The intersection of a row and a column is called a **cell**. A table may be created from scratch or can be assembled from preexisting text.

Do It!

Juan wants to insert a table into his and Sabrina's report.

1. Open the file **Report2** from your student disk. This is the copy of Sabrina and Juan's report, which you were working on in the last lesson.

2. Place the insertion point at the end of the second paragraph, after the word "home."

3. Insert a **manual page break**. (There will not be enough room on the page for the table without it.) The insertion point will appear just below the new break.

4. Click the **Insert Table** button ▦ on the Standard toolbar. A table grid appears, allowing you to choose the number of rows and columns in your table.

5. Move the mouse pointer over the table grid until a **2 x 3** area is selected, as shown in Figure 4-1, and click. A table appears in the document at the insertion point with gridlines delineating the rows and columns, and cell markers showing the end of the text in each cell, as shown in Figure 4-2. If the cell markers are not showing, you can make them appear by clicking ¶ on the Standard toolbar.

Figure 4-1 Using the Insert Table button

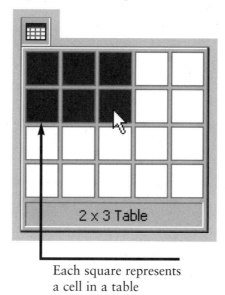

Each square represents
a cell in a table

Figure 4-2 Creating a blank table in a document

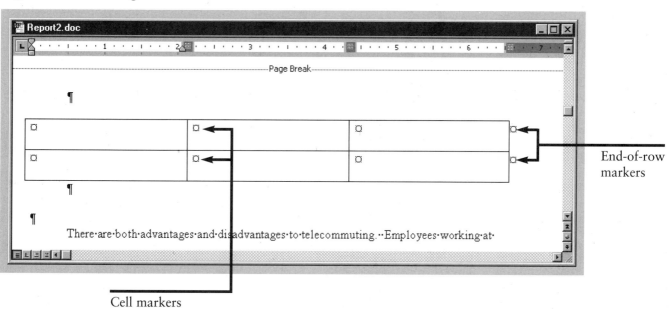

End-of-row
markers

Cell markers

Creating Tables

(continued)

Do It!

6 Type the following three pieces of information, pressing [Tab] once after each of the first two:

      Occupation   Total   Percent at Home

7 Press [Tab] to go to a new line.

8 Type the following three pieces of information, pressing [Tab] once after each of the first two:

      Managerial   14.4   5.2

Your table should now resemble the one in Figure 4-3.

More

You can also create a table by selecting existing text in your document and clicking the Insert Table button; the cells in the table will be determined by the tabs and paragraphs in the selection. A new table may also be created manually by clicking Table, then clicking Draw Table. The Tables and Borders toolbar (see Figure 4-4) will appear, and you can draw a table and its row and column borders using the mouse pointer. From the Insert Table dialog box you may also access the **AutoFormat** dialog box, which will be explained later in the lesson.

If you wish to insert an existing worksheet into your Word document, you can insert it as a **linked object** or an **embedded object**. A linked object will show up in the Word document (its **destination file**) but will remain linked to its source file, and any changes made to the source file will be reflected in the destination file. If it is inserted as an embedded object, the file will become part of the Word document and can be altered by double-clicking it to open the parent application. This is an excellent example of the way different Microsoft Office Applications can be used together productively. For example, if you have an Excel worksheet that is being updated frequently and you would like to insert it into your Word document as a table, inserting it as a linked object means that you can be sure that the table will always be up to date. To insert a linked object at the insertion point, click Insert, then click Object, then click the Create from File tab. Select the file you wish to insert, and select the Link to file check box. (If this box is not checked, the file will be inserted as an embedded object instead.) The table will appear in your Word document, and double-clicking it opens an Excel window from which it can be fully edited. Word's Help facility offers many more tips and methods for fully utilizing these functions.

Figure 4-3 Adding information to a table

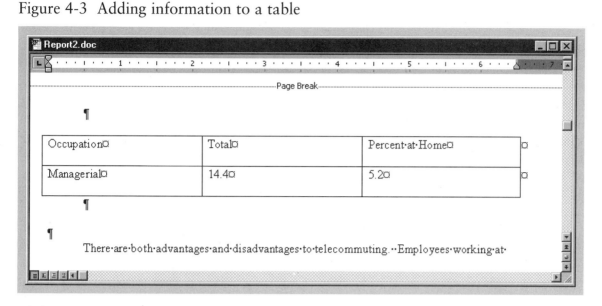

Figure 4-4 Tables and Borders toolbar

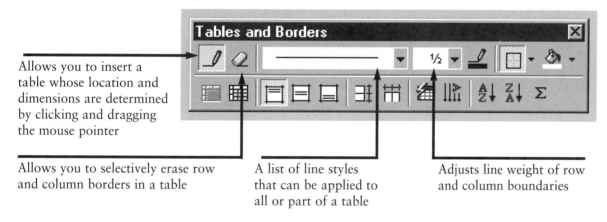

Allows you to insert a table whose location and dimensions are determined by clicking and dragging the mouse pointer

Allows you to selectively erase row and column borders in a table

A list of line styles that can be applied to all or part of a table

Adjusts line weight of row and column boundaries

Practice

To practice creating tables, open the student file **Prac4-1**.

Hot Tip

You can create a new Word table with Microsoft Excel by clicking the **Insert Microsoft Excel Worksheet** button 🔳 on the Standard toolbar. Then you can use all the Excel commands within that worksheet to create your table.

Editing Tables

Concept

A table in a Word document can be edited in much the same way that ordinary text is edited.

Do It!

Juan would like to change the "Total" heading in his table to "Total (in millions)" and "Percent at Home" to "Percent Working at Home."

1 Position the insertion point just after the word "Total" in the table.

2 Type a space, then type (**in millions**) to complete the heading.

3 Press [**Tab**] to move to the next cell to the right. All the information in the cell will be selected.

4 Click between the words "Percent" and "at" to deselect the cell and position the insertion point there.

5 Type **Working** and press [**Space**] to complete the cell.

More

As you can see, table editing is very similar to editing text in a paragraph. Text may be centered or aligned to either side of a cell by selecting it and clicking the appropriate formatting button. Also, the selection bar works in much the same way in a table as it does with text. Clicking in the selection bar next to a row selects the entire row; dragging up or down in the selection bar adds more rows to the selected area. In addition, there is a miniature selection bar area at the left end of each cell, and clicking it will select the entire cell. A cell may also be selected by triple-clicking it, whereas double-clicking will select an entire word just as it does in regular text. To select a column, place the mouse pointer over its top boundary until the mouse pointer changes to a downward arrow ↓, then click to select the column. Cells can be made wider or narrower by clicking and dragging their edges: Place the mouse pointer on the gridline that makes up the edge of a cell until it changes to ↔, then click and drag the cell to the desired length. If you click and drag the edge of a selected cell, then that cell will be the only one in its column to be affected. To make the whole column's width change, make sure that no cells are selected before you adjust the edges.

The insertion point may be placed anywhere in a table with the mouse pointer, or the keyboard may be used in a variety of ways to move through the table and select its contents. Table 4-1 shows many keyboard movement and selection techniques that will make working with tables much easier. Remember to press [Tab] instead of [Enter] to move to the next cell; pressing [Enter] causes a new line to be created within the cell. When the insertion point is within the boundaries of a table, the ruler will reflect the table's column boundaries. (See Figure 4-5.) Dragging the column boundary markers on the ruler will change the corresponding column widths. When exact precision is required, row and column sizes may be manually entered in the Cell Height and Width dialog box, available on the Table menu.

Table 4-1   Keyboard Movement and Selection Shortcuts

Desired Action	Press This
Move to the next or previous cell in a table and select its contents	[Tab] or [Shift]+[Tab]
Move up or down one row	[↑] or [↓]
Move to the first or last cell in a row	[Alt]+[Home] or [Alt]+[End]
Move to the top or bottom cell in a column	[Alt]+[Pg Up] or [Alt]+[Pg Dn]
Select an entire column	[Alt]+Click
Select an entire table	[Alt]+[5] on the numeric keypad (with Num lock off)

Figure 4-5 Formatting a table using the ruler

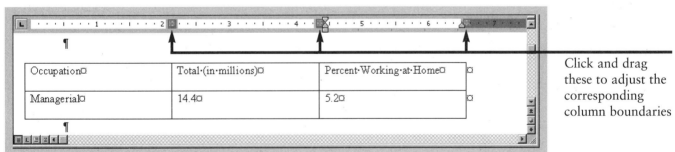

Click and drag
these to adjust the
corresponding
column boundaries

Inserting and Deleting Rows and Columns

Concept

Word makes it easy to add or delete rows and columns in a table when more or fewer are required.

Do It!

Juan wants to add three rows of new data to the table.

1. Position the insertion point in the last cell in the last row of the table, after the number 5.2.

2. Press [Tab]. The insertion point moves to the first cell of a new row.

3. Type the following nine pieces of information, pressing [Tab] between each:

Professional	15.5	4.9
Sales	13.2	6.2
Service	14.9	3.7

   The entered text is automatically formatted to fit into three new rows.

More

To insert additional empty rows or columns, first select the row or column that will be moved down or over to accommodate the new one. Then click the Insert Rows button or the Insert Columns button, which will appear in place of the Insert Table button when a row or column is selected. The number of new rows or columns created is the same as the number selected. For example, if you select two rows and click the Insert Rows button, two new empty rows will appear above the ones you selected. To add a column to the end of a table, select the end-of-column markers in the same way you would select a column, then click the Insert Columns button. To delete a row or column, select it and then right-click it. The **Table shortcut** menu (Figure 4-6) will appear, offering, among other choices, an option to delete your selection. You can also use this menu to insert additional columns or rows. The Table shortcut menu has many of the same commands available on the Table menu, as well as shortcuts to several standard formatting dialog boxes, such as Font and Paragraph. Row and column dimensions may also be adjusted from the **Cell Height and Width** dialog box (Figure 4-7), available on the Table menu.

Figure 4-6 Table shortcut menu

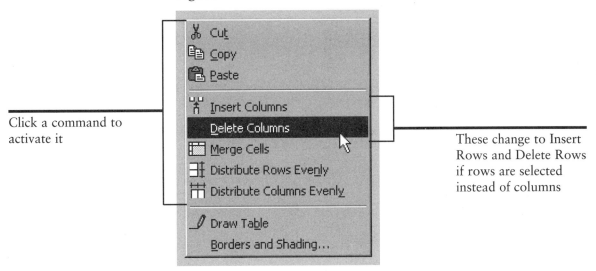

Click a command to
activate it

These change to Insert
Rows and Delete Rows
if rows are selected
instead of columns

Figure 4-7 Cell Height and Width dialog box

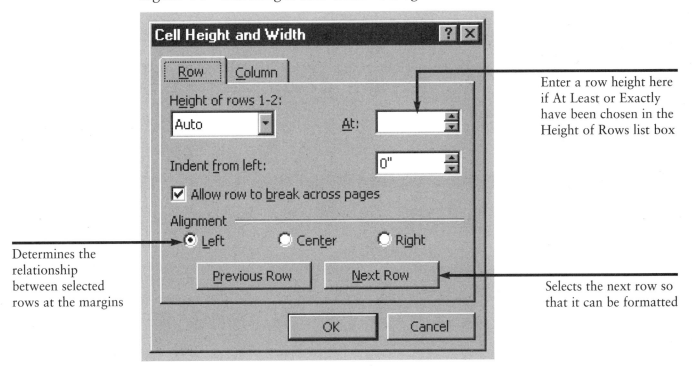

Enter a row height here
if At Least or Exactly
have been chosen in the
Height of Rows list box

Determines the
relationship
between selected
rows at the margins

Selects the next row so
that it can be formatted

Practice

To practice inserting and deleting rows and
columns, open the student file **Prac4-3**.

Hot Tip

To easily delete an entire row or column,
select it and then either use the cut command or press **[Shift]+[Delete]**. Just pressing [Delete] will leave the cells intact but
erase the contents.

Sorting Data in a Table

Concept

Cells in a Word table can be automatically **sorted** by various criteria without re-typing them or going through tedious cutting and pasting. For example, Word can automatically alphabetize a long table of names or sort a table of orders by shipping date.

Do It!

Juan would like his table to list occupations in order of decreasing Working-at-Home percentage.

1. Make sure the insertion point is positioned inside the table.

2. Click **Table**, then click **Sort**. The Sort dialog box appears, as shown in Figure 4-8.

3. Click the **Sort by** drop-down list arrow, then click **Percent Working at Home**. Word automatically reads all your column headings and includes them in the list, with the first heading as the default choice. When Percent Working at Home was chosen, Word analyzed the kind of data in that column and changed the **Type** list box from text to number.

4. Click the **Descending** radio button in the Sort By section to make Word sort the table with the largest values first.

5. Click the **Header Row** radio button in the My List Has section if it is not already selected.

6. Click [OK] to sort the table. The rows are placed in descending order according to their value in the Percent Working at Home column.

More

Word allows you to sort by more than one criterion. For example, if you had a table of names with people's first and last names in separate cells, Word could sort them primarily by last name, then by first name. Thus, if several people had the same last name, Word could sort them by first name as well. Word allows up to three levels of sorting in this fashion. You can set secondary sorting criteria on the Sort dialog box by choosing another criterion in the Sort by text box. In the My List Has section, the default setting is **Header Row**, meaning the first row of your table explains the contents of the cells below, such as the header "Occupation" in Juan's table. If you select **No Header Row**, Word will make the first row into labels such as Column 1, Column 2, and so on. Also, if No Header Row is chosen but you do in fact have a header row, your column titles will be sorted with the other rows and may not end up at the top of the table.

Since only one row in Juan's table actually needed to be relocated, he could have moved the row manually. An alternative to the sort feature is to select an entire row and then move it with the pointer, the same way you move regular text. Release the dragged text in the row that you want to end up beneath the selection being moved.

Figure 4-8 Sort dialog box

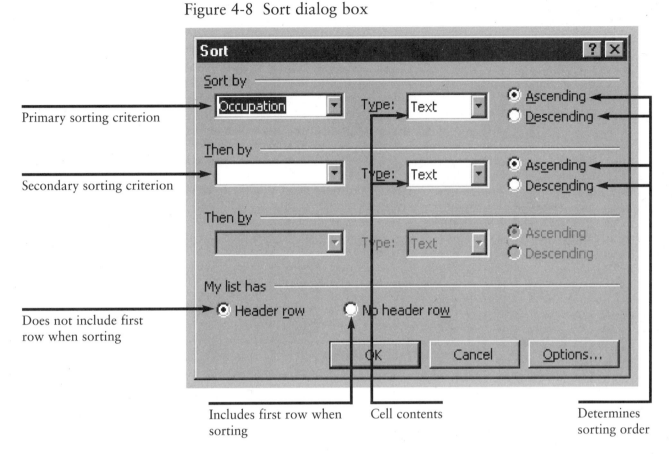

Primary sorting criterion

Secondary sorting criterion

Does not include first
row when sorting

Includes first row when
sorting

Cell contents

Determines
sorting order

Practice

To practice sorting data in a table, open the
student file **Prac4-4**.

Hot Tip

You can make Word sort uppercase and
lowercase letters differently by clicking the
Case Sensitive check box in the Sort
Options dialog box, available by clicking
Options... in the Sort dialog box.

Calculating Data in a Table

Concept

The **Formula** command makes it easy to perform calculations with data in a table. Word comes with several formulas such as sums, products, and averages, but additional formulas may be entered to meet the needs of each user.

Do It!

Juan wants Word to automatically average the values in the Percent Working at Home column and insert the average in a new cell.

1. Position the insertion point after the number 3.7 in the last cell of the last row of the table.

2. Press [**Tab**] to create a new row.

3. Type the word **Average** into the first cell of the new row.

4. Press [**Tab**] twice to move the insertion point to the last cell in the row.

5. Click **Table**, then click **Formula**. The Formula dialog box appears, as shown in Figure 4-9, with the formula =SUM(ABOVE) suggested in the Formula text box.

6. Delete the suggested formula by selecting it and pressing [**Delete**].

7. Click the **Paste Function** list arrow, then click **AVERAGE**. The AVERAGE formula appears in the Formula text box with the insertion point between parentheses.

8. Type **C2:C5**, the range of cells you wish to average, in between the parentheses.

Figure 4-9   Formula dialog box

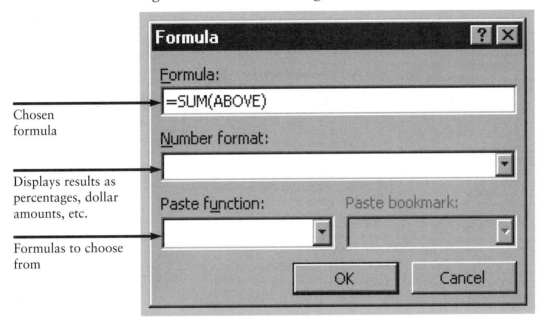

Chosen
formula

Displays results as
percentages, dollar
amounts, etc.

Formulas to choose
from

Calculating Data in a Table (continued)

Do It!

9 Place the insertion point before the word "AVERAGE" in the Formula text box.

10 Press [=] to place an equal sign before the formula. The equal sign at the beginning tells Word that a formula, rather than a label or a value, is about to be entered.

11 Click [OK] to apply the formula to the column. The average of the values in the column, 5, appears in the last cell of the table, as shown in Figure 4-10.

More

Changing data in one of the cells that the calculation is based on does not immediately affect the result seen on the screen. To update the calculation taking the new data into account, select the column that has to be recalculated and press [**F9**], which is the **Update Fields** command.

When entering your own formulas into the Formula dialog box you will refer to other cells in the table using cell references, which identify a cell by its position as a function of its column letter and row number. For example, the cell reference for the second cell in the third column is C2. (See Figure 4-11.) You can use the Word Formula feature in many ways. In Figure 4-12, formulas are used to calculate the total monthly spending for three different people as well as the resulting 12-month projected total cost. The formulas shown are the ones that would be entered into the Formula text box when the Formula dialog box is called up with the insertion point in that particular cell. Each of the formulas in the Monthly Total column (Column E) adds the numbers to the left in their respective rows to arrive at the total. Likewise, the formulas in Column F multiply by 12 the monthly total for the row that was just calculated to arrive at a projected total for the year. The symbol for multiplication is an asterisk (*); division is represented by a slash (/). As they are in Figure 4-12, the formulas will result in an unformatted number. To make the calculated result appear with a dollar sign and two decimal places showing, click the Number Format text box in the Formula dialog box, and then click $#,##0.00;($#,##0.00) on the drop-down list. This will be tacked on to the end of the formula in the Formula text box, which will instruct Word to place the result in the correct format.

Figure 4-10 Appearance of table with calculated average

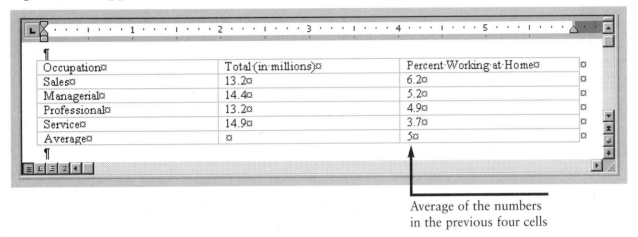

Occupation¤	Total·(in·millions)¤	Percent·Working·at·Home¤	¤
Sales¤	13.2¤	6.2¤	
Managerial¤	14.4¤	5.2¤	
Professional¤	13.2¤	4.9¤	
Service¤	14.9¤	3.7¤	
Average¤	¤	5¤	

Average of the numbers
in the previous four cells

Figure 4-11 Cell references

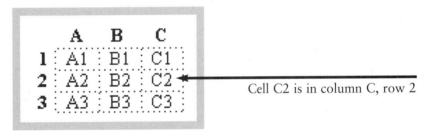

	A	B	C
1	A1	B1	C1
2	A2	B2	C2
3	A3	B3	C3

Cell C2 is in column C, row 2

Figure 4-12 Sample table with formulas in the cells to which they will be applied

¤	Rent/month¤	Food/month¤	Other/Month¤	Monthly·Total¤	Annual·Total¤
Margot¤	$450¤	$65¤	$340¤	=SUM(LEFT)¤	=E2*12¤
Bart¤	$625¤	$125¤	$385¤	=SUM(LEFT)¤	=E3*12¤
Diane¤	$900¤	$95¤	$290¤	=SUM(LEFT)¤	=E4*12¤

This formula adds all values
to the left in its row to get the
monthly total

This formula multiplies
the contents of cell E4
by 12 to get the annual
total

Practice

To practice calculating data in a table, open the student file **Prac4-5**.

Hot Tip

Word has several different preset formulas and number formats available to you on the drop-down lists in the Formula dialog box, or you can enter your own into the Formula and Number Format text boxes.

Formatting a Table

Concept

A table's appearance can be changed in many ways. Word's **table formatting** options include, among others, shading, borders, and 3-D effects.

Do It!

Juan wants to format his table to improve its appearance.

1 Place the insertion point after the space after the word "Total" and press **[Enter]**.

2 Place the insertion point after the space after the word "Working" and press **[Enter]**.

3 Click and drag the column edges to approximately match the column widths in the table in Figure 4-13.

4 Select columns **B** and **C**.

5 Click the **Center** alignment button on the Formatting toolbar. Word centers the selected columns.

6 Select the entire table, then press **[Ctrl]+[1]** (use the number keys above the keyboard, not the numeric keypad) to single-space the text.

7 After deselecting the columns by clicking elsewhere in the table, place the insertion point in the table and click **Table,** then click **Table AutoFormat**. The Table AutoFormat dialog box appears with a sample table in its **Preview** box, as shown in Figure 4-14.

8 Scroll down in the **Formats** list box and click **Grid8**. The Preview box shows the characteristics of this table format.

9 Click the **Last Row** check box in the **Apply Special Formats To** section at the bottom of the Table AutoFormat dialog box. This will visually differentiate your last row from the others, indicating that it contains a different type of information from the other rows.

10 Click [OK] to close the dialog box and apply the specified formatting to your table. It changes from a simple line grid enclosing text to a clean, professional-looking table. (See Figure 4-14.)

More

You can explore the various formatting options available to you in the Table AutoFormat dialog box by selecting various formats and options and viewing the results in the Preview box. If your table spans more than one page and it has a header row to explain the contents of the columns, you can instruct Word to put the heading at the top of each new page of the table. To do so, place the insertion point in the header (first) row. Click **Table,** then click **Headings**.

Figure 4-13 Finished table

Occupation	Total (in millions)	Percent Working at Home
Sales	13.2	6.2
Managerial	14.4	5.2
Professional	13.2	4.9
Service	14.9	3.7
Average		**5**

Figure 4-14 Table AutoFormat dialog box

List of table formats to choose from

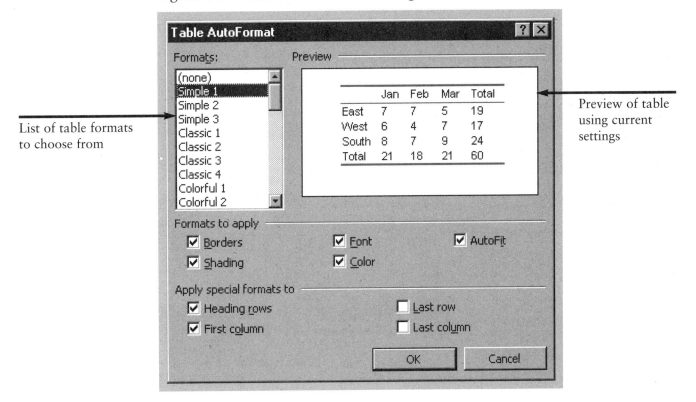

Preview of table using current settings

Practice

To practice formatting a table, open the student file **Prac4-6**.

Hot Tip

Borders applied to a row are moved with it when rows are sorted. Therefore, you should always sort a table before formatting it with Table AutoFormat, or the table could be formatted incorrectly.

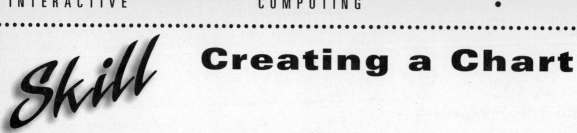

Creating a Chart

Concept

Sometimes a table may be more readily understood if it is presented graphically as a **chart**.

Do It!

Juan wants to display his table as a chart.

1. Place the insertion point anywhere within the table.

2. Click **Table,** then click **Select Table** to select the entire table.

3. Click **Insert,** then click **Object.** The Object dialog box appears.

4. Scroll down through the **Object Type** box and double-click **Microsoft Graph 97 Chart.** It opens, turning your table into a Microsoft Graph Datasheet, as shown in Figure 4-15. A preliminary chart appears, based on Juan's data and the program's defaults.

5. Click **Chart,** then click **Chart Options.** The Chart Options dialog box appears with the Titles tab on top.

6. Type **Home-Based Workers** into the **Chart title** text box. After a brief delay, the title will appear at the top of the preview chart.

7. Press [**Tab**] to move the insertion point to the the **Category (X)** text box, then type **Occupation.** After a brief delay, it will appear at the bottom of the preview chart.

8. Click [OK] to create the chart.

9. Close the Datasheet window. The chart you have created appears below Juan's table in a hatched frame, as shown in Figure 4-16. Some parts of the chart, especially the labels beneath it, appear cramped and cut off. These will be fixed in the next Skill. Notice that when the chart is selected, positioning the mouse pointer over a column of the chart brings up a ScreenTip displaying both what series the column represents and its exact value.

10. Click the blank area on the right-hand side of the page to deselect the chart.

More

The Chart Type dialog box, available on the Chart menu, has an extensive repertoire of formats to choose from. The Microsoft Graph application automatically suggests the type of graph or chart that seems to most closely match the format of your data, as all formats are not appropriate for all situations. For example, Juan's table could not be accurately or effectively expressed with a pie chart or radar graph.

Figure 4-15   Chart datasheet created from a table

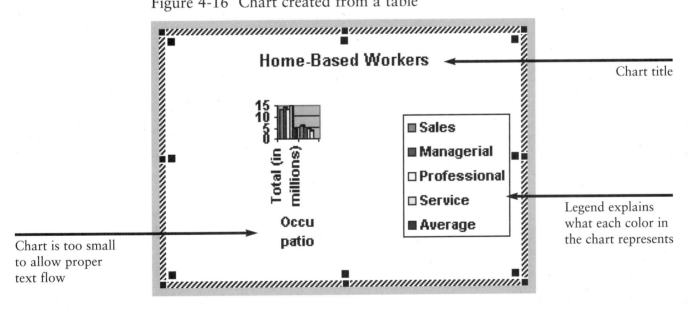

Shows what color will
represent what data in
the chart

Figure 4-16   Chart created from a table

Chart title

Legend explains
what each color in
the chart represents

Chart is too small
to allow proper
text flow

Practice

To practice creating a chart, open the student file **Prac4-7**.

Hot Tip

If the proper files have been installed on your computer, you can use the **Help** feature of Microsoft Graph 97 Chart to find out more about its various capabilities in the same way that you use Word's Help.

Changing a Chart

Concept

Word treats a chart as a graphic object instead of as text, but it may still be modified by accessing the program that created it.

Do It!

Juan is dissatisfied with the appearance of his chart, especially its size and its column labels. He wants to fix these problems and remove the Average column from the chart entirely.

1 Double-click the chart to open **Microsoft Graph**. The Microsoft Graph toolbar will replace the Standard and Formatting toolbars at the top of the screen, and a hatched frame will appear around the chart with sizing handles at its corners and at the midpoint of each side.

2 Click the midpoint sizing handle on the bottom of the chart's frame, drag it downward and release it just below the 4 1/2" mark on the vertical ruler. The chart expands vertically, making it possible for more increments to appear along the vertical axis of the chart.

3 Click the midpoint sizing handle on the right side of the frame, then drag the edge of the frame to the right and release it when it is even with the 5 1/2" mark on the horizontal ruler. The chart expands horizontally until it is almost the width of the page, and has room to display the column labels along the bottom without breaking them up awkwardly.

4 Click the **Average** column on the chart. (It is the column farthest to the right.) Dots appear in the corners to indicate that it is selected.

5 Press [**Delete**]. The Average column disappears and the chart is automatically updated, removing its reference from the legend and expanding the other columns slightly to make up for the space left behind by its removal. The chart should now look like the one in Figure 4-17.

6 Save and close the document.

More

When working with a chart in a Word document, remember that the chart is a foreign element created by another application. To make changes to the chart itself, you must first double-click it to open its parent application. To alter a chart based on changed data in the table that the chart was created from, you must either alter the data sheet for the table, available on the View menu of the Graph program, or recreate the chart. To act upon the chart as an element of your Word document (that is, move it or copy it to another document), only click it once to select it. A box indicated by sizing handles, not the hatched frame that indicates that its parent application has been opened, will appear around it. Then you may cut the chart and paste it, or move it by dragging it and dropping it to another location within the document. Text added during chart creation, such as the title and category, may be changed by selecting it and entering new text. When selected, a frame will appear around it indicating its selection.

Figure 4-17 Properly modified chart

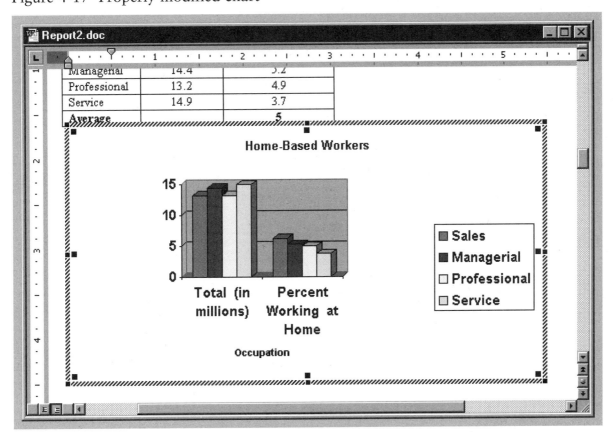

Shortcuts

Function	Button/Mouse	Menu	Keyboard
Insert a table	⊞	Click Table, then click Insert Table	
Insert a row above the selected row	Right-click the selected row, then click Insert Rows (Or click ⊞)	Click Table, then click Insert Rows	
Insert a column to the left of the selected column	Right-click the selected column, then click Insert Columns (Or click ⊞)	Click Table, then click Insert Columns	
Delete the selected row	Right-click the selected row, then click Delete Rows	Click Table, then click Delete Rows	[Shift]+[Delete]
Delete the selected column	Right-click the selected column, then click Delete Columns	Click Table, then click Delete Columns	[Shift]+[Delete]
Align selected text in a cell or paragraph to the left	▤		[Ctrl]+[L]
Align selected text in a cell or paragraph to the right	▤		[Ctrl]+[R]
Center selected text in a cell or paragraph	▤		[Ctrl]+[E]
Justify selected text in a cell or paragraph	▤		[Ctrl]+[J]

Identify Key Features

Figure 4-18 Identifying components of a table

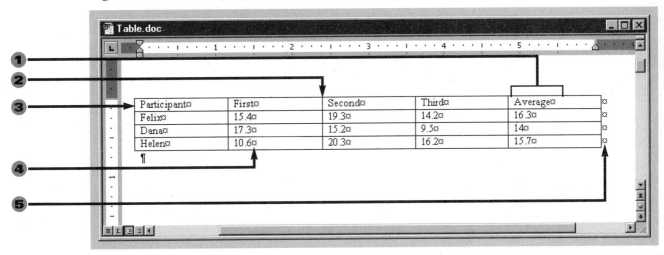

Select the Best Answer

6. Indicates a selected chart

7. An order in which data can be sorted

8. Appears when you right-click a table

9. Explains the symbols and colors being used in a chart

10. Visible boundary between cells in a basic table

a. Descending

b. Gridlines

c. Table shortcut menu

d. Hatched border

e. Legend

Quiz (continued)

Complete the Statement

11. The Insert Table command:

    a. Creates a table based on the Normal template

    b. Creates a table based on dimensions you choose

    c. Pastes data from the Clipboard into a table

    d. Replaces the desktop with a tabletop

12. To move the insertion point to the next cell in the current row:

    a. Press [End]

    b. Use the right arrow key on the keyboard

    c. Press [Tab]

    d. Double-click the table

13. D14 refers to:

    a. The fourteenth cell in the fourth column

    b. The fourteenth cell in the fourth row

    c. A formula

    d. A document designation for a Word table

14. Paragraphs and table columns both have:

    a. Page numbers

    b. Selection bars

    c. Gridlines

    d. Sorting features

15. The first step in creating a chart from a selected table is:

    a. Clicking the Chart button

    b. Pressing [Ctrl]+[F8]

    c. Clicking Insert, then clicking Chart

    d. Clicking Insert, then clicking Object

16. The Chart legend:

    a. Is about the ChartWizard

    b. Must be created in Excel and inserted into the Word document containing the chart it belongs with

    c. Contains the Color buttons

    d. Explains the meaning of colors used in the chart

Interactivity

Test Your Skills

1. Open a new document and create a table:

   a. Open a new Word document.

   b. Click Table, then click Insert Table to bring up the Insert Table dialog box.

   c. Create a table that is 4 rows by 5 columns.

2. Add data to the table:

   a. Enter a name into each of the lower three cells in the leftmost column.

   b. Insert a number between 1 and 100 into each of the three cells to the right of each name, for a total of nine cells.

   c. Label the cells in the top row as follows: **Name, March, April, May,** and **Average.**

3. Average the columns and sort the table:

   a. Position the insertion point in the second cell down in the last column, which is cell E2.

   b. Click Table, then click Formula to open the Formula dialog box.

   c. Enter the formula **=AVERAGE(B2:D2)** into the Formula text box and press [Enter].

   d. Repeat the last three steps for the other two cells in the Average column, making sure that you are using the correct cell references for the appropriate calculation.

   e. Sort the table in the order of descending Average.

4. Format the table:

   a. Place the insertion point within the table and click Table, then click Table AutoFormat.

   b. Select a table format that you like and check the boxes that you want in the Formats to Apply section of the dialog box.

   c. Make sure that both the Heading Rows and First Column check boxes are checked in the Apply Special Formats To section of the dialog box and press [Enter].

   d. Save the document to your student disk as **Test 4.**

Interactivity (continued)

Problem Solving

Using the skills you learned in Lesson 4, create a chart from the table in the document **Test 4**, which you made in the previous section. Accept the default Chart type, and try to make the chart clear and precise. When you have finished modifying the chart, save the document to your student disk as **Solved 4**.

L E S S O N

ADVANCED FORMATTING

Once you have learned the basic elements of formatting, you can utilize some of Word's more advanced formatting options. With a little practice, you will be able to create documents with columns, lists, and drop caps. Word also allows you to achieve greater flexibility in designing documents by letting you break documents up into sections with fundamentally different formatting.

When creating more complex Word documents, you may wish to insert an item such as a graphic or a placed text box. Word lets you add such features in different ways to fulfill varying design purposes. A graphic can be inserted directly into text as if it were a large letter, or you can add a frame to it that lets you position it on the page independent of text. A section of text can be placed on the page in the same way, overlapping other text or set between lines.

Word also makes it possible to shrink a document slightly to make it fit into a smaller number of pages without going back and manually adjusting the line spacing, font size, or margins.

Case Study:
Juan has written the text of a club newsletter, but has not yet formatted it into the configuration he wants. In this lesson, you will help him format part of the newsletter in columns, create bulleted and numbered lists, and add graphics and framed text items. When finished, it will be shrunk to fit on a single page and then printed.

Formatting Text with Columns

Concept

Word makes it easy to format text into multiple parallel **columns** running down the page. Two, three, or even more columns may be used, with text freely flowing between them as it is edited.

Do It!

Juan wants to format the text he has written for a newsletter into three columns.

1. Open the student file **Doit5-1** and save it on your student disk as **Newsletter.doc**.

2. Select all of the text in the document by clicking just before the word "The" at the beginning and dragging to just after the word "scale" at the end. The blank lines before and after the text should not be selected.

3. Click **Format**, then click **Columns** to bring up the Columns dialog box, as shown in Figure 5-1.

4. Click the **Three** option in the **Presets** box. A blue border will appear around it indicating its selection and the sample document in the Preview box will change from one to three columns.

5. Click the **Line Between** check box above the Preview Box. Lines will appear between the columns in the Preview box.

6. Click OK to apply these formatting changes to the document. Word will automatically switch to Page Layout View so you can view the three columns as they will actually appear on the page. Leave the document open, as you will be using it throughout the lesson.

More

Selected text can be quickly formatted into up to six columns by clicking the **Columns** button 🔳 on the Standard toolbar and dragging down and to the right to select the desired number of columns. (See Figure 5-2.) When the insertion point is in a section that is in column format, the ruler reflects the column boundaries. These boundary markers may be moved by clicking on their edges and dragging if you do not wish to go to the Columns dialog box. In many senses, each column in a multi-column document acts like a normal, single-column document. For example, columns can be formatted with any of the text alignment options available in a normal document, and text wrapping occurs in columns just as in a normal document. In addition, just as the selection bar runs down the left side of a single-column document, the left side of each column in a multi-column document contains its own selection bar to select lines of text in that column.

Figure 5-1 Columns dialog box

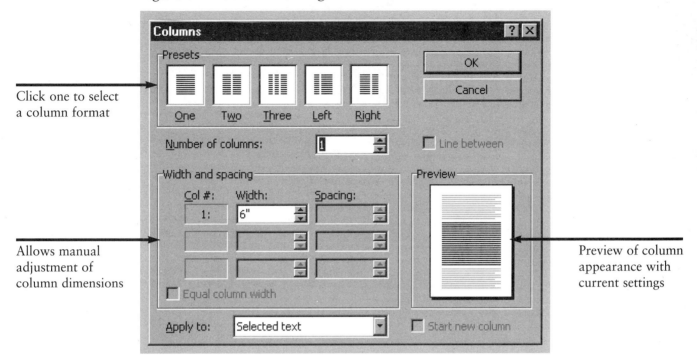

Click one to select
a column format

Allows manual
adjustment of
column dimensions

Preview of column
appearance with
current settings

Figure 5-2 Using the Columns button on the
Standard toolbar

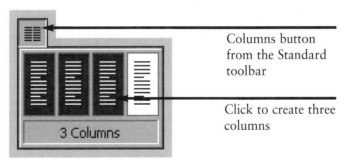

Columns button
from the Standard
toolbar

Click to create three
columns

3 Columns

Practice

To practice formatting text with columns,
open the student file **Prac5-1**.

Hot Tip

Unless the print is very small, it is usually
not a good idea to format text into more
than three columns on a vertically oriented
page, as the text wrapping becomes erratic
and the columns become difficult to read.

Making Bulleted and Numbered Lists

Concept

Bulleted and numbered lists can be created quite easily in Word. A **bullet** is a dot or other marker used to delineate separate items in a list when their sequence is unimportant. **Numbers** can be used in any list but are often used to indicate a sequence of events.

Do It!

Juan wants to arrange the three upcoming projects into a numbered list and also wants to add bullets to the list of newly elected officers.

1 Select the second, third, and fourth paragraphs in the first column of the document, from "Adopting a 3-mile section..." to "...late this spring."

2 Click the **Numbering** button ▤ on the Formatting toolbar. Word will automatically indent the three paragraphs and number them consecutively, as seen in Figure 5-3.

3 Select the four lines, split between the second and third columns, that list the new officers. Remember that pressing [Shift] allows you to add to a selection after releasing the mouse button.

4 Click the **Bullets** button ▤ on the Formatting toolbar. The names and positions are automatically indented and bullets appear in front of each one.

More

When a selected piece of text is formatted into bulleted or numbered lists, one bullet or number will automatically be assigned to each paragraph. Once inserted, a bullet or number is not part of the text, and it cannot be selected. It can, however, be deleted, and in the case of a numbered list, the list will correct itself so that there is no gap between consecutive numbers. For example, if item 7 in a list is deleted, all numbers in the list higher than 7 will decrease by one so that the list does not go from 6 to 8. To remove bullets or numbers from lists you have already created, simply select the list and click either the Numbering or Bullets button, whichever matches the selected text, to remove the formatting.

The **Bullets and Numbering** dialog box, available on the Format menu, gives you more flexibility in choosing the options you want. (See Figure 5-4.) You can choose various kinds of bullets or different numbering methods. Word also allows you to use a standard indent instead of the default hanging indent if you prefer. A hanging indent indents all lines after the bullet or number the same amount; turning off this option makes additional lines of the list item appear directly beneath the bullets or numbers instead of lining up with the indent.

Word can also create a numbered or bulleted list while you enter the information. If you type the first item of such a list after the number 1, for example, Word will automatically format the list with a hanging indent and start the next line with the number 2 when you press [Enter]. Once created, this list behaves just like a list that has been created manually. This feature is called the **AutoFormat As You Type** option and it also formats such items as common fractions and ordinals (1st, 2nd, 3rd, etc.) as you type.

Figure 5-3 Automatic formatting of a numbered list, before (left) and after

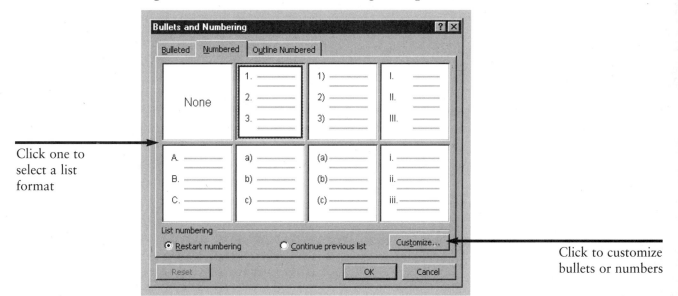

Adopting·a·3-mile·section·of· Route· 47· and· organizing· a· litter·cleanup·twice·a·month¶
Participation· in· National· Air· Pollution· Awareness· Week· activities¶
Putting· on· a· composting· seminar· out· by· the· greenhouses·late·this·spring.¶

1. Adopting·   a·   3-mile· section·of·Route· 47· and· organizing·   a·   litter· cleanup·twice·a·month¶
2. Participation· in· National· Air·Pollution· Awareness· Week·activities¶
3. Putting·on· a· composting· seminar·   out·   by·   the· greenhouses·   late·   this· spring.¶

Word breaks the selection into numbered items at the paragraph marks

Figure 5-4 Bullets and Numbering dialog box

Click one to select a list format

Click to customize bullets or numbers

Practice

To practice making bulleted and numbered lists, open the student file **Prac5-2**.

Hot Tip

The AutoFormat As You Type option can be customized from the AutoFormat and AutoFormat As You Type tabs of the AutoCorrect dialog box, available on the Tools menu.

Adding Borders and Shading

Concept

Borders and shading can be used to make a document more visually appealing. **Borders** are lines that are added above, below, to either side, or all around selected paragraphs to set them apart from their surroundings. **Shading** is a background color or pattern that can be applied behind paragraphs to draw attention to them.

Do It!

Juan wants to add shading to his topic headings and a border around the meeting announcement in his newsletter.

1. Select the bold heading Awareness Update in the first column by clicking next to it in the selection bar.

2. Click **Format,** then click **Borders and Shading**. The Borders and Shading dialog box appears, as shown in Figure 5-5.

3. Click the **Shading** tab to bring it to the front.

4. Click the **20%** option in the **Style** list box. The Preview box will display a 20% density shading.

5. Click [OK] to apply the shading to the selected text.

6. Select the second bold heading in the document, **Recycling News,** by clicking next to it in the selection bar of its column.

7. Press **[Ctrl]+[Y]** (the Repeat/Redo command) to apply the last command to the selected text. Word automatically applies the same shading to the new heading.

8. Repeat steps 6 and 7 for the other two bold headings in the document, first **New Officers!** and then **Meeting Notice**. They should end up shaded like the first two headings.

9. Now press **[Ctrl]+[Shift]+[↓]** to add the paragraph following **Meeting Notice** to it within the selected area.

10. Click the **Tables and Borders** button ⊞ on the Standard toolbar. The Table and Borders toolbar appears.

11. Click the **Line Weight** list arrow on the Tables and Borders toolbar, then click 1 ½ pt.

12. Click the **Border** drop-down list arrow ⊞▾ and then select the outside border button ⊞ The selected text appears within the specified border.

More

When creating a border, you can choose lines of varying thickness and styles. The border can be applied to any side of the text using either the Borders tab of the Borders and Shading dialog box or the various buttons on the Table and Borders toolbar. The Table and Borders toolbar, shown in Figure 5-6, controls almost every option available from the dialog box.

Figure 5-5 Borders and Shading dialog box

Click one to choose a
border type

Click a border
style to select it

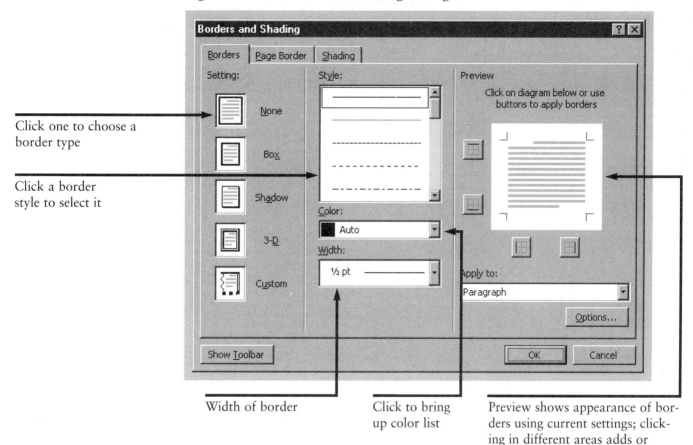

Width of border

Click to bring
up color list

Preview shows appearance of borders using current settings; clicking in different areas adds or
deletes sections of the border

Figure 5-6 Tables and Borders toolbar

Click to bring up the line
style drop-down list

Outside border

Click to add or remove
a border from a side

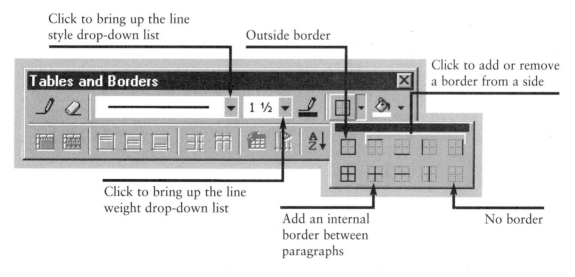

Click to bring up the line
weight drop-down list

Add an internal
border between
paragraphs

No border

Practice

To practice applying borders and shading,
open the student file **Prac5-3**.

Hot Tip

You can change the color of borders and
shading from the Borders and Shading dialog box; shades will still be expressed in
terms of density percentage, or mixture of
background and shading color.

Adding a Drop Cap
to a Paragraph

Concept

In many publications, such as books and magazines, the first letter of a paragraph is often much larger than those in the surrounding text. This letter is called a **drop cap**. Word makes it quite easy to add a drop cap to a document, with a variety of options available to fit the user's needs.

Do It!

Juan wants to format the first paragraph of his newsletter with a drop cap.

1. Place the insertion point within the first paragraph of the newsletter.

2. Click **Format**, then click **Drop Cap**. The Drop Cap dialog box appears, as shown in Figure 5-7.

3. Click the **Dropped** option in the **Position** section. A blue border will appear around it indicating its selection.

4. Click `OK` to change the first letter of the paragraph into a drop cap, which appears in a frame.

5. Click elsewhere in the document to deselect the drop cap. Your document should now resemble Figure 5-8.

More

When added to a paragraph, a drop cap appears in a frame. You can select it and change its font and style as desired, and it may be moved or resized easily by dragging it or by adjusting its sizing handles. Using the sizing handles at the midpoints of its sides will stretch the box containing the drop cap, while using one of the corner sizing handles will expand or shrink the box while retaining the original aspect ratio, or proportions.

Figure 5-7 Drop Cap dialog box

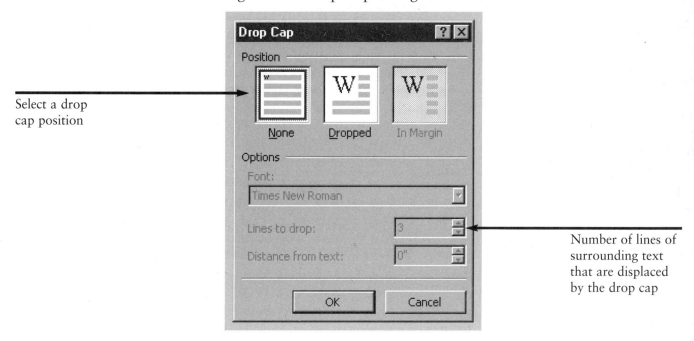

Select a drop
cap position

Number of lines of
surrounding text
that are displaced
by the drop cap

Figure 5-8 Juan's newsletter formatted with a drop cap

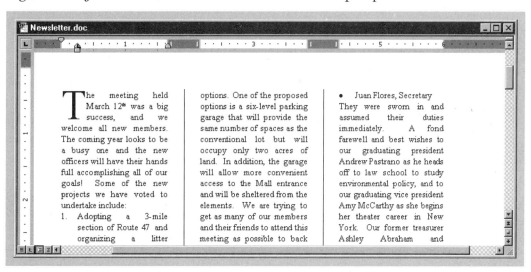

Practice

To practice formatting paragraphs with drop
caps, open the student file **Prac5-4**.

Hot Tip

Drop caps are ordinarily used only once per
major section, not at the beginning of every
paragraph.

Working with Sections and Section Breaks

Concept

A **section break** is the boundary between two **sections** in a document. Sections are helpful when two or more parts of a document require different formatting, such as a different number of columns.

Do It!

Juan wants to make the last paragraph of the newsletter stretch across the bottom of the page in a single wide column.

1 Position the insertion point at the beginning of the last paragraph of the document, just before "The Local Environment...."

2 Click **Insert**, then click **Break**. The Break dialog box appears, as seen in Figure 5-9.

3 Click the **Continuous** radio button in the **Section Breaks** section.

4 Click [OK] to insert the break. The last paragraph is now split among the three columns at the bottom of the document.

5 Press [Enter] to add a blank line separating the text from the preceding columns.

6 Select the last paragraph, whose beginning is now near the bottom of the first column, by clicking just before "The Local Environment..." in the selection bar and dragging straight down to select the rest of the paragraph and the remaining blank lines in the document.

7 Click the **Columns** button 🔲 on the Standard toolbar, then click the leftmost column in its drop-down box. The selected paragraph is formatted into a single column stretching from margin to margin. (See Figure 5-10.)

More

When you first formatted the newsletter into three columns, a section break should have appeared before and after the selected text, as blank lines at the beginning and end still retained their original single-column formatting. Word will automatically insert a section break when column formatting is changed in only part of a document. As you learned in Lesson 3, section breaks can also be used to separate distinct parts of a single document, such as chapters in a book or articles in a magazine. The different sections do not necessarily have to have different formatting, but treating them as separate sections makes it easier to work with them within the scope of a large document.

Figure 5-9 Break dialog box

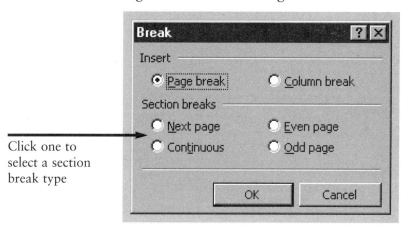

Click one to
select a section
break type

Figure 5-10 Juan's newsletter formatted with a section break

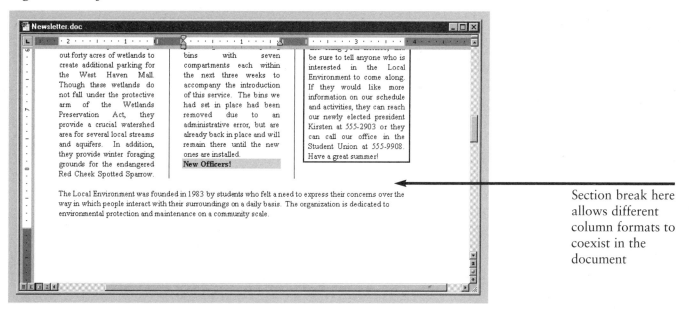

Section break here
allows different
column formats to
coexist in the
document

Practice

To practice working with sections and section breaks, open the student file **Prac5-5**.

Hot Tip

If you cannot see the section break, click the Show/Hide button ¶ on the Standard toolbar.

Adding Graphics to a Document

Concept

To make a document more interesting to read, **graphics** can be added to it. Word can import a variety of graphics formats and it offers many ways to modify the graphic once it is part of a Word document.

Do It!

Juan wants to add a picture to the top of his newsletter and resize it to fit.

1 Press [Ctrl]+[Home] to place the insertion point at the beginning of the document.

2 Press [Enter] to insert a blank line.

3 Click **Insert**, then select **From File** from the **Picture** submenu. The Insert Picture dialog box appears.

4 From this dialog box, find and select the student file **Doit5-6**. A preview of the selected graphic will appear in an area at the right of the dialog box.

5 Click [Insert] to insert the graphic into the newsletter at the insertion point.

6 Click the graphic to select it. Sizing handles and the Picture toolbar appear. If you do not see the Picture toolbar, turn it on by selecting the **Toolbars** command from the View menu, and then clicking **Picture**.

7 Click the **Format Picture** button [icon] on the Picture toolbar.. The Format Picture dialog box appears.

8 Click the size tab to bring it to the front of the dialog box. (See Figure 5-11.)

9 Change the contents of the **Height** box in the **Scale** section from 100 to 24. Word will add the % symbol for you. Make sure that **Lock aspect ratio** is checked. Click once in the dialog box to automatically change the width to match the height.

10 Click [OK] to reformat the picture. The picture shrinks to its new size. The newsletter should now look like Figure 5-12.

More

A simpler way to insert a graphic into a document is to paste it in at the insertion point from the Clipboard. However, Word treats a graphic imported in this fashion as a text object, and it becomes more difficult to manipulate the graphic. Graphics that have been properly inserted using the Insert Picture command can be resized by clicking and dragging the sizing handles that appear when the graphic is selected. Use the corner sizing handles to maintain the graphic's original proportions.

You can also **crop** an image, or hide portions of it. To do so, click the Crop button on the Picture toolbar. The mouse pointer will change to the **cropping tool** 占, and and clicking and dragging a sizing handle toward the center of the graphic will cause only the portion inside the dragged border to appear when the mouse button is released. Dragging away from the center of the graphic with the cropping tool until the border is larger than the graphic itself will cause the extra space to be incorporated into the image. Cropping is reversible, in that Word remembers the original image and can crop it again to show more or less of it at any time.

Figure 5-11 Format Picture dialog box

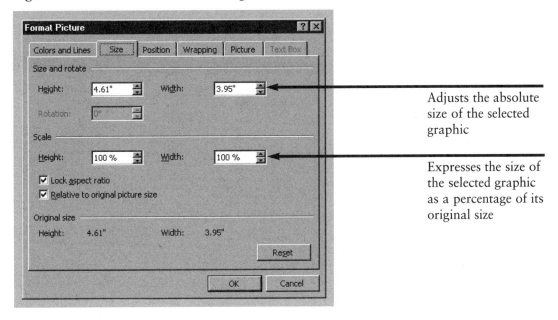

Adjusts the absolute size of the selected graphic

Expresses the size of the selected graphic as a percentage of its original size

Figure 5-12 Graphic inserted into Juan's newsletter

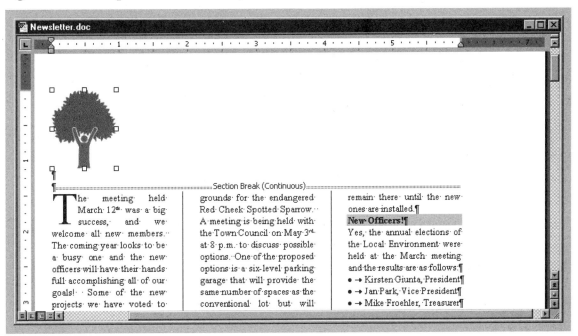

Practice

To practice adding graphics to a document, open the student file **Prac5-6**.

Hot Tip

Moving an inserted graphic can be accomplished by clicking it and dragging, just as you would move a block of selected text. Word will insert it into a line of text at the insertion point.

 **Inserting Graphics into Text**

Concept

Graphics can be placed within the text of a document Once inserted into the body of the document, they can be manipulated easily to interact with the text in the most appropriate manner.

Do It!

Juan would like to insert a recycling symbol graphic into his newsletter at the beginning of the Recycling News section.

1 Place the insertion point just before the word "Many" under the Recycling News heading in the newsletter.

2 Click **Insert,** then select **Picture** and choose **From File** from the submenu. As before, the Insert Picture dialog box appears.

3 Find and select the student file **Doit 5-7.** A preview of the recycling graphic will appear in a square at the right of the dialog box.

4 Click ⬚ Inse**r**t ⬚ to insert the picture into the newsletter at the insertion point.

5 Click on the graphic to select it. Sizing handles and the Picture toolbar appear.

6 Click the **Format Picture** button 🖉 on the Picture toolbar. The Format Picture dialog box opens.

7 Click the **Size** tab.

8 In the Size and rotate section, change the **Height** to **0.58"** and the **Width** to **0.64"**. If the **Lock aspect ratio** check box is checked, it is only necessary to change one.

9 Click ⬚ OK ⬚ to resize the graphic.

10 While the graphic is still selected, click the **Text Wrapping** button 🔲 on the Picture toolbar. From the menu that appears, click **Square**.

11 Click once away from the graphic. Your document should look like Figure 5-13.

More

A graphic can also be placed behind text as a background. This kind of graphic is called a **watermark,** and can be produced as follows: Insert a graphic and select it as you normally would. On the Picture toolbar click the **Image Control** button 🔳. A pop-up menu will appear with four choices. Click the last choice, **Watermark,** to automatically remove contrast from the graphic. Then click the Text Wrapping button on the Picture toolbar and choose **None**. This will allow the text to appear in front of the graphic. If the graphic overpowers the text, you can lighten it even more with the Less Contrast button 🔳 on the Picture toolbar.

Figure 5-13 Graphic inserted into Juan's newsletter

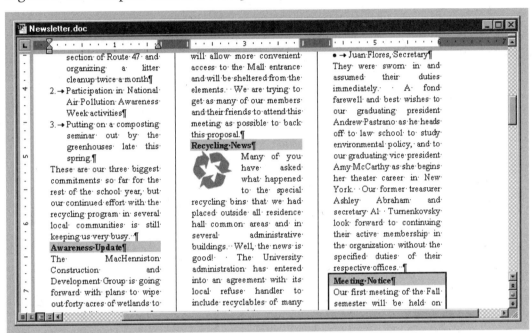

Using Text Boxes

Concept

When text is entered inside a text box, it can be sized and positioned much like a graphic.

Do It!

Juan wants to add a previously formatted masthead to his newsletter.

1 Open the student file **Doit5-8.**

2 Press [Ctrl]+[A] to select the entire document.

3 Click **Insert,** then click **Text Box.** A frame will appear around the block of text.

4 Click the middle sizing handle on the right side of the text box and drag it to the 5-inch mark on the horizontal ruler.

5 Press [Ctrl]+[C] to copy the framed text to the Clipboard.

6 Close the document. Do not save changes. The newsletter reappears in the active window.

7 Position the insertion point at the left end of the section break line appearing at the top of the newsletter. (If you cannot see the break, you can make it appear by clicking the **Show/Hide** button ¶ on the Standard toolbar.)

8 Press [Ctrl]+[V] to paste the text into the newsletter at the insertion point. It appears within a rectangular border over the inserted tree graphic and the top of the newsletter, as shown in Figure 5-14.

9 Click the middle sizing handle on the bottom of the text box and drag it up until it is even with the middle sizing handles on the sides of the frame. Then release the mouse button.

Figure 5-14 Masthead in a text box inserted into Juan's newsletter

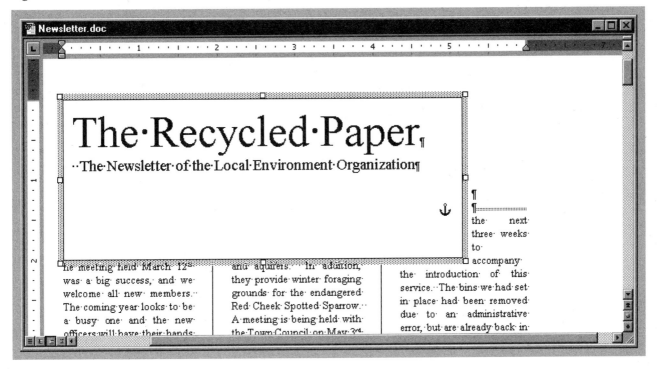

 **Using Text Boxes**

(continued)

Do It!

10 Choose **Text Box** from the Format menu to bring up the Format Text Box dialog box.

11 Click the **Colors and Lines** tab if it is not already on top.

12 Click the **Color** drop-down list in the Line section, then click [No Line].

13 Click [OK] to close the dialog box. The border around the text will disappear when the text box is deselected.

14 Click the frame to select it again (but not on a sizing handle) and drag it into place next to the tree graphic. After deselecting the relocated frame, the document should resemble Figure 5-15.

15 Press [Ctrl]+[Home] to move the insertion point to the beginning of the document.

16 Press [Delete] twice to eliminate the two blank lines at the beginning of the document. The insertion point is now positioned at the left end of the section break at the top of the page.

More

Positioning a text box is similar to positioning a graphic. Resizing, however, is slightly different. When the width of a frame containing text is reduced, the text rewraps as if the edges of the frame were margins. Reducing the height of the frame just cuts off the text that could not fit inside it. The text size will not change when the frame size is altered.

When a text box is created or selected, the Text Box toolbar (Figure 5-16) will appear. If it does not, it can be found on the View menu under Toolbars. The Text Box toolbar offers useful tools for working with text inside a text box and for working with multiple text boxes. The Create Text Box Link button 🔗 allows you to link text boxes, making text flow between them as it is edited. Once boxes have been linked, you can use the Break Forward Link button 🔗 to sever the link between them. You can use the Next Text Box and Previous Text Box buttons to move between linked text boxes quickly.

Figure 5-15 Juan's newsletter with masthead text box inserted and moved into place

Figure 5-16 Text Box toolbar

Create or break a link
between text boxes

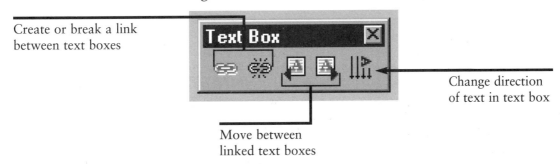

Change direction
of text in text box

Move between
linked text boxes

Practice

To practice manipulating text with text
boxes, open the student file **Prac5-8.**

Hot Tip

Text in a text box can still be edited and
formatted normally. Just place the insertion point in the framed text or select it to
delete a word, change the font, or alter it in
any way you would normally modify text.

 **Shrinking a Document to Fit**

Concept

If a small portion of a document does not fit on a page, Word can automatically shrink aspects of the document such as text size and line spacing until it reduces the number of total pages, thereby eliminating the "widow" of leftover text at the top of the extra page.

Do It!

Juan wants to fit his newsletter onto a single page and print it out.

1 Click the **Print Preview** button 🖺 on the Standard toolbar. The Print Preview screen comes up, with the newsletter appearing on two pages If you do not see two pages, click the Multiple Pages button 🖽 and select 1 x 2 pages.

2 Click the **Shrink to Fit** button 🖼 on the Print Preview toolbar. The document is shrunk and appears on one page.

3 Juan notices that shrinking the document has moved the recycling graphic out of place. Click the graphic with the magnification tool to zoom in on it, and then click the Magnifier button on the toolbar to turn it off.

4 Click the recycling graphic to select it.

5 Press the down arrow key 10 times to move the graphic back into place.

6 Juan scrolls down the page and also notices that the "New Officers!" heading is now in the last row, and he decides to correct it.

7 Place the insertion point just after the line above the "New Officers!" heading.

8 Press [Enter] to move the heading to the top of the next column. When demagnified, the document should now look like Figure 5-17. If the preview shows a blank second page, click the Multiple Pages button and select 1 x 1 pages.

9 Click Close to exit the Print Preview screen.

10 Click the **Print** button 🖨 on the Standard toolbar, making sure that the computer is properly connected to a working printer. The newsletter is finished!

More

When attempting to shrink a document, Word will only change certain aspects of the document, and then only to a certain degree. If too much text is on the final page to allow Word to comfortably shrink the document, it will notify you that it was unable to complete the command and will leave the document unchanged. Sometimes, especially with longer documents, the Shrink To Fit command can remove several pages from the total number of pages in the document.

Figure 5-17 Juan's finished newsletter, shrunk to fit on one page

The Recycled Paper
The Newsletter of the Local Environment Organization

The meeting held March 12ᵗʰ was a big success, and we welcome all new members. The coming year looks to be a busy one and the new officers will have their hands full accomplishing all of our goals! Some of the new projects we have voted to undertake include:

1. Adopting a 3-mile section of Route 47 and organizing a litter cleanup twice a month
2. Participation in National Air Pollution Awareness Week activities
3. Putting on a composting seminar out by the greenhouses late this spring.

These are our three biggest commitments so far for the rest of the school year, but our continued effort with the recycling program in several local communities is still keeping us very busy.

Awareness Update

The MacHenniston Construction and Development Group is going forward with plans to wipe out forty acres of wetlands to create additional parking for the West Haven Mall. Though these wetlands do not fall under the protective arm of the Wetlands Preservation Act, they provide a crucial watershed area for several local streams and aquifers. In addition, they provide winter foraging grounds for the endangered Red Cheek Spotted Sparrow. A meeting is being held with the Town Council on May 3ʳᵈ at 8 p.m. to discuss possible options. One of the proposed options is a six-level parking garage that will provide the same number of spaces as the conventional lot but will occupy only two acres of land. In addition, the garage will allow more convenient access to the Mall entrance and will be sheltered from the elements. We are trying to get as many of our members and their friends to attend this meeting as possible to back this proposal.

Recycling News

Many of you have asked what happened to the special recycling bins that we had placed outside all residence hall common areas and in several administrative buildings. Well, the news is good! The University administration has entered into an agreement with its local refuse handler to include recyclables of many types in its pickups around campus. They will be providing their own recycling bins with seven compartments each within the next three weeks to accompany the introduction of this service. The bins we had set in place had been removed due to an administrative error, but are already back in place and will remain there until the new ones are installed.

New Officers!

Yes, the annual elections of the Local Environment were held at the March meeting and the results are as follows:
• Kirsten Giunta, President
• Jan Park, Vice President
• Mike Froehler, Treasurer
• Juan Flores, Secretary

They were sworn in and assumed their duties immediately. A fond farewell and best wishes to our graduating president Andrew Pastrano as he heads off to law school to study environmental policy, and to our graduating vice president Amy McCarthy as she begins her theater career in New York. Our former treasurer Ashley Abraham and secretary Al Turnenkovsky look forward to continuing their active membership in the organization without the specified duties of their respective offices.

Meeting Notice

Our first meeting of the Fall semester will be held on September 2ⁿᵈ at 7 o'clock in the Robert J. Lamson Auditorium. So come along and bring your friends, and be sure to tell anyone who is interested in the Local Environment to come along. If they would like more information on our schedule and activities, they can reach our newly elected president Kirsten at 555-2903 or they can call our office in the Student Union at 555-9908. Have a great summer!

The Local Environment was founded in 1983 by students who felt a need to express their concerns over the way in which people interact with their surroundings on a daily basis. The organization is dedicated to environmental protection and maintenance on a community scale.

Practice

To practice shrinking a document to fit into the space available, open the student file **Prac5-9**.

Hot Tip

The Shrink To Fit command can often be used more than once to further reduce the size of a document.

Shortcuts

Function	Button/Mouse	Menu	Keyboard
Format selected text into columns	▦	Click Format, then click Columns	
Create a bulleted list from selected paragraphs	☰	Click Format, then click Bullets and Numbering; Go to the Bullets tab	
Create a numbered list from selected paragraphs	☰	Click Format, then click Bullets and Numbering; Go to the Numbering tab	
Apply borders	▣	Click Format, then click Borders and Shading	
Apply shading	▣	Click Format, then click Borders and Shading	
Insert section breaks		Click Insert, then click Break	
Adjust size of a picture	Drag sizing handles to the dimensions you want	Click Format, then click Picture	
Shrink a document to fit	▣ (From the Print Preview Screen)		
Change direction of text in a text box	▥ (From the Text Box toolbar)	Click Format, then click Text Direction	

Identify Key Features

Figure 5-18 Identifying advanced formatting features

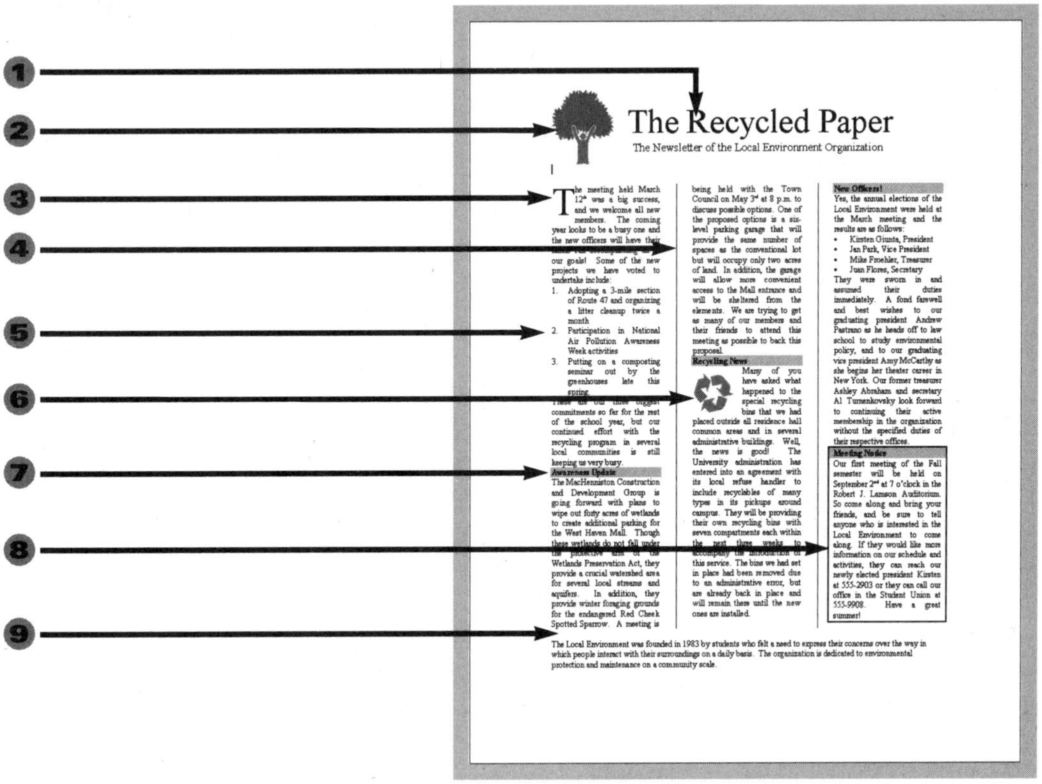

Select the Best Answer

10. It is expressed as a percentage of a color

11. A letter that is much larger than the text surrounding it

12. A character used to demarcate separate items on a list

13. An inserted item that allows different column formats to coexist in one document

14. Minutely reduces line spacing, font size, and other formatting characteristics in an attempt to reduce the space taken up by a document's text

15. Squares that can be clicked and dragged to alter the dimensions of an inserted object

a. Drop cap

b. Shrink to Fit command

c. Bullet

d. Sizing handles

e. Shading

f. Section break

Quiz (continued)

Complete the Statement

16. A section break must be inserted between passages of text with different:

    a. Font sizes

    b. Bullets

    c. Margins

    d. Column formats

17. Hiding part of a graphic is called:

    a. Scrubbing

    b. Marking

    c. Cropping

    d. Cutting

18. Lines of different colors and styles that can be inserted around paragraphs are called:

    a. Margins

    b. Borders

    c. Section Breaks

    d. Frames

19. The text formatting option that is not normally available on the Formatting toolbar is:

    a. Align left

    b. Outline

    c. Font Color

    d. Bold

20. The [■] button:

    a. Brightens dark documents

    b. Copies the selection to the Clipboard

    c. Shifts the text down and to the right

    d. Shrinks a document

21. The anchor icon:

    a. Is embedded in the bottom of the page

    b. Keeps a graphic from moving when its frame is changed

    c. Appears next to the paragraph mark for the paragraph the frame is associated with

    d. Indicates that text flow has been disabled

Interactivity

Test Your Skills

1. Open a document of text and format it with a bulleted list:

    a. Open the student file **SkillTest 5** and save it to your student disk as **Test 5**.

    b. Select the four items following the second paragraph, after "...on the block:"

    c. Format the four selected lines into a bulleted list.

2. Add shading and drop caps to the document:

    a. Select the entire document.

    b. Apply a 10% shade to the selected area.

    c. Place the insertion point in the first paragraph.

    d. Format the paragraph with a standard drop cap using Word's default settings.

    e. Format the second and last paragraphs with a standard drop cap as well.

3. Add a graphic to the document:

    a. Place the insertion point at the end of the document.

    b. Click Insert, then click From File from the Picture submenu to open the Insert Picture dialog box.

    c. Insert the graphic labeled as the student file SkillTest 5a into the document.

    d. Click and drag the graphic onto the first page of the document if it isn't there already.

    e. Right-click the graphic, then click Format Picture to bring up the Format Picture dialog box.

    f. From the Position tab of the dialog box, make the Horizontal position 4" relative to the Page, and make the Vertical position 0" relative to the Paragraph. The graphic should take up the entire right side of the page, and the text should flow down the left side.

Interactivity (continued)

Problem Solving

Using the skills you learned in Lesson 5, create the document below. Open the student file **Problem Solving 5** and save it as **Solved 5** on your student disk. When you have finished, the document should contain a section break between two different column formats, two drop caps, a bulleted list of four items, a text box, and a graphic inserted as a watermark. The text for the text box at the top may be obtained from the student file **Problem Solving 5a**. The graphic for the watermark may be obtained from the student file **Problem Solving 5b**. When you have finished, save and close the document.

Figure 5-19 Final appearance of Solved 5

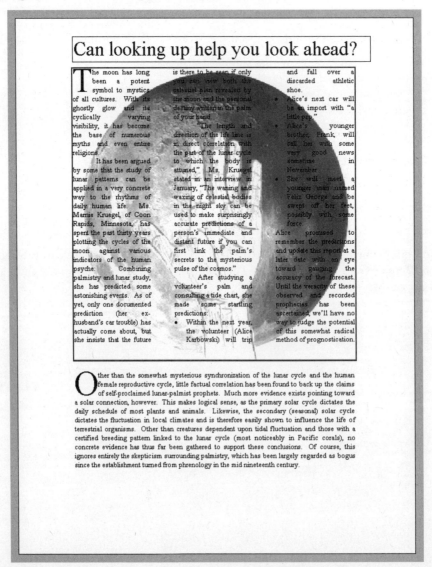

Skills

LESSON 6

MERGING DOCUMENTS

Sometimes it is necessary to create a large number of similar documents, such as form letters or billing statements. Instead of having you create these documents individually, Word allows you to create a single document plus a separate file containing the information that will be unique to each copy when it is printed. This powerful feature, known as Mail Merge, makes large-scale mailings and other similar chores as simple as creating a letter and an address list.

Once you have made a list of recipients' names and addresses, called a data source, you can use it again for a different form letter or to create addressed envelopes and mailing labels, or you can simply print the information out as a table.

Case Study:
Juan is mailing the newsletter he created in Lesson 5 to some members of the Local Environment Club. He is going to create a form letter and a list of recipients, and then he will specify where in the letter each person's information will be placed. Finally, he will merge the letter and data together, print out all copies of the form letter, and create mailing labels to get the newsletters and form letters to their destinations.

Creating
a Main Document

Concept

Before documents can be merged, a **main document** must be created. This document consists of all the elements of the letter that will be common to all copies, called **boilerplate text**; it can be made out of any standard Word document.

Do It!

Juan wants to create a main document from a letter he has written to go along with his newsletter.

1 Open the document **Doit6-1** and save it as **MainDoc** on your student disk. This is the form letter that Juan has written.

2 Click **Tools**, then click **Mail Merge**. The Mail Merge Helper dialog box appears, as shown in Figure 6-1.

3 Click [Create ▾], then click **Form Letters**. A dialog box appears asking where to get the text for the form letter.

4 Click [Active Window]. The dialog box disappears and the document name is displayed in the Main Document section of the Mail Merge Helper dialog box. The letter has now been transformed into a main document. The Mail Merge Helper dialog box will remain open.

More

A mail merge document consists of several basic elements. You have already learned about boilerplate text, the text common to all copies of a merged document. A **data source** is the table-like document created to hold all the **fields** that will be inserted into a merged document, such as name, address, date, salary, or any other kind of information that will be inserted into the final document. The fields in a data source are grouped by **record**, one record for each item or individual that the record's fields pertain to. For example, the data source for a merged document from a politician to his or her constituents would contain one record for each person on the mailing list, and each record would contain several fields for each person. The **header row** in a data source contains the names of the fields.

Figure 6-1 Mail Merge Helper dialog box

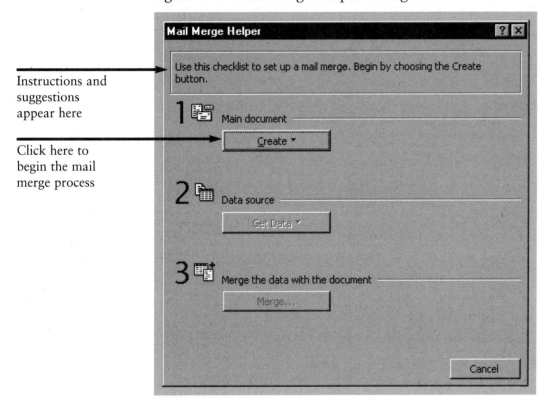

Instructions and suggestions appear here

Click here to begin the mail merge process

Practice

There is no practice file for this Skill, as an additional Word file cannot be opened with the Mail Merge Helper dialog box open.

Hot Tip

It doesn't matter if your document does not fill an entire page; Word inserts a section break after each merged copy to force the next copy to start on the next page.

Creating a Data Source

Concept

Once a main document has been created, a data source can be created and linked to the main document. A previously existing data source may be used, or a new one may be created. Before records can be entered into a new data source, its fields must be defined.

Do It!

Juan wants to create a data source for his form letter.

1. Click [Get Data ▾], then click **Create Data Source**. The Create Data Source dialog box appears, as shown in Figure 6-2. Word offers many common field titles, and Juan must delete the ones he does not require.

2. Click **Title** in the **Field Names in Header Row** section, then click [Remove Field Name]. The selected field is removed from the list. Now the rest of the unneeded field names must be removed.

3. Repeat step 2 to remove these additional field names: **JobTitle**, **Company**, **Address2**, **Country**, **HomePhone**, and **WorkPhone**. Now Juan wants to add one field name that was not included in the list.

4. Replace the selected contents of the **Field Name** text box with **GradYear**.

5. Click [Add Field Name ▸▸] to add the new field name to the end of the list.

6. Click [▴] four times (slowly) to move the GradYear field name up the list to just after the LastName field. Now the field names are in the proper order.

7. Click [OK]. The Save As dialog box appears with the insertion point in the File Name box.

8. Type **Merge Data** into the File Name box. Make sure that you are saving into the same folder that the main document is associated with.

9. Click [Save]. A message box appears telling you that no records are in the data source. Don't click anything yet; they will be added in the next Skill.

More

A data source may consist of a single record or may contain hundreds. The fields in a data source can be anything that will differ in each version of the final merged document, whether it be a single word, such as a salutation, or an entire paragraph. The flexibility of Word's Mail Merge feature is what makes it so useful for creating large numbers of similar documents.

Figure 6-2 Create Data Source dialog box

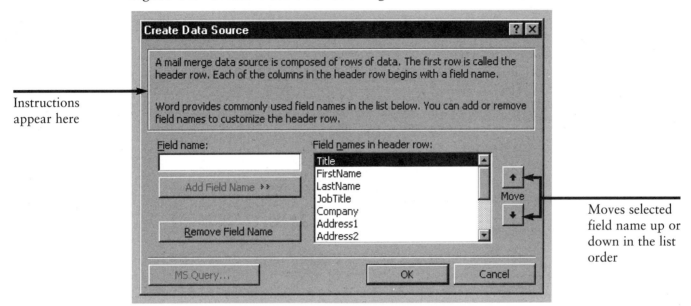

Instructions
appear here

Moves selected
field name up or
down in the list
order

Practice

There is no practice file for this Skill, as an
additional Word file cannot be opened with
the Mail Merge Helper dialog box open.

Hot Tip

A data source may be shared by several
merged documents.

 **Adding Information to a Data Source**

Concept

Once a data source has been created and its fields specified, records can be added.

Do It!

Juan wants to add records to the data source.

1 Click [Edit Data Source] in the Microsoft Word message box. The Data Form dialog box appears with the insertion point in the FirstName field, as shown in Figure 6-3.

2 Type **Diane**, then press **[Enter]**. The text you entered appears in the **FirstName** field and the insertion point moves to the next field.

3 Type **Holdorf** into the **LastName** field, then press **[Enter]**.

4 Type 90 into the **GradYear** field, then press **[Enter]**.

5 Type **336 E. 18th St.** into the **Address1** field, then press **[Enter]**.

6 Type **Minneapolis** into the **City** field, then press **[Enter]**.

7 Type **MN** into the **State** field, then press **[Enter]**.

8 Type 55404 into the **PostalCode** field.

9 Click [OK] to accept the data and close the Data Form dialog box. (If you were adding more records, you would have clicked [Add New] instead.) The main document reappears in the active window with the **Mail Merge** toolbar (see Figure 6-4) underneath the Formatting toolbar.

More

When the last field in a particular record has been filled, the next blank record may be opened by pressing [Enter] instead of clicking [Add New]. If you wish to undo a change to the record, click [Restore]; the record will be restored to its original state. Fields may be left blank for some records without disrupting the mail merge process. For example, if the fields you have created include middle names and one is not known for an individual, Word will automatically leave a blank space where the missing data would have appeared in the final merged document.

Figure 6-3 Data Form dialog box

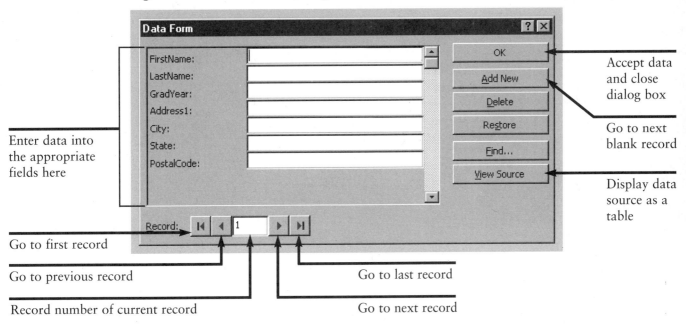

Enter data into
the appropriate
fields here

Accept data
and close
dialog box

Go to next
blank record

Display data
source as a
table

Go to first record

Go to previous record

Record number of current record

Go to last record

Go to next record

Figure 6-4 Mail Merge toolbar

Brings up list of selected
fields to choose from

Click to bring up the
Mail Merge Helper
dialog box

Edit data source

Practice

To practice adding information to a data
source, open the student file **Prac6-3**.

Hot Tip

You can quickly edit your data source at
any point by clicking the **Edit Data Source**
button 🖉 on the Mail Merge toolbar to
return to the Data Form dialog box.

 **Adding Merge Fields to a Main Document**

Concept

A **merge field** tells Word what data to insert and where to insert it into a main document when merging. A merge field appears as the field name that will be inserted enclosed in chevrons. (See Figure 6-5.)

Do It!

Juan wants to designate data from an existing data source for use with his form letter, and he wants to insert the merge fields into his main document.

1 Click the **Mail Merge Helper** button ⊞ to bring up the Mail Merge Helper dialog box again.

2 Click [Get Data ▾] , then click **Open Data Source**.

3 Select the student file **Doit6-4**. This is the data source containing the names and addresses on Juan's mailing list for the form letter.

4 Click [Open] to open the file. A Microsoft Word dialog box appears saying that the file MergeData has not been saved and asking if you want to save it.

5 Click [No] . A preexisting data source will be used in the final merge instead. A Microsoft Word dialog box appears saying that no merge fields have been inserted into the main document.

6 Click [Edit Main Document] . The main document reappears in the active window.

7 Select the words **recipient's address** underneath the graphic.

8 Click [Insert Merge Field ▾] , then click **FirstName**. The field appears at the insertion point.

9 Press [**Space**]. A dot appears marking the space. As you can see, inserting merge fields requires a combination of merge fields from the drop-down list and keystrokes.

10 Insert the rest of the fields and keystrokes as follows: **LastName** [Space] ['] **GradYear** [Enter] **Address1** [Enter] **City** [,] [Space] **State** [Space] [Space] **Postal Code**.

11 Double-click the word **recipient** below the fields you have just entered to select it.

12 Click [Insert Merge Field ▾] , then click **FirstName**. The field appears at the insertion point. The fields you have inserted should look like those in Figure 6-5.

13 Click the **Save** button 🖫 on the Standard toolbar to save the main document with the merge fields that have been inserted.

More

When the document is merged, the information specified by each merge field will be added to replace the name of the field as it appears in the main document. Merge fields can be inserted anywhere in a main document, and may be formatted in any way that text can be formatted. For example, formatting the merge field in italics will italicize the inserted data in the final merged document.

Figure 6-5 Proper placement of merge fields in Juan's form letter

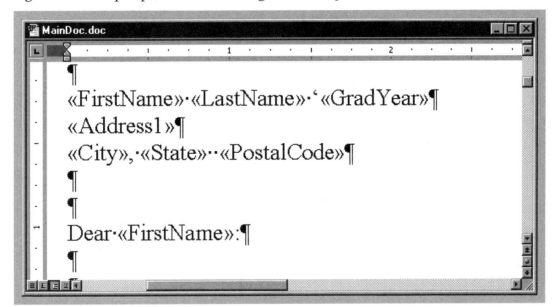

Practice

To practice adding merge fields to a main document, open the student file **Prac6-4**.

Hot Tip

Merge fields can also be used effectively within the main body of the letter. For example, Juan could have added a field for "Major" and then written, "What did you end up doing with your <<Major>> degree?"

Editing Individual Merged Documents

Concept

Merged documents based on a single main document and containing the same fields of information can still be **personalized**. Once the document has been merged, different copies of the document can be easily edited to meet the user's needs.

Do It!

Juan wants to merge the documents and personalize one of them.

1 Click the **Merge to New Document** button on the Mail Merge toolbar. The main document and data source are merged into a new document called Form Letters1 that consists of several pages, each page a letter based on the main document with a record's data inserted in the merge fields.

2 Place the insertion point after the word "input" in the second-to-last sentence in the letter, before the period. There is a copy of the letter on every page; make sure that you are on the first page, in the letter addressed to Diane Holdorf.

3 Type **, and let us know how Eric and Felix are doing**. The sentence should now read "Please give us a call and share your input, and let us know how Eric and Felix are doing." (See Figure 6-6.)

More

Once the files have been merged, they are transformed into one long document consisting of all copies of the letter that will eventually be printed. At this point the new document may be treated like any other Word document, and individual letters in it may be modified normally.

If many records will be used, it may be unwieldy to create a single file containing all copies of the document. Clicking the **Merge To Printer** button on the Mail Merge toolbar prints out all copies of the merged document without first creating a bulky file containing all of them. This makes it impossible to edit individual documents or to preview them, however. To merge only specified records with the main document instead of merging all the records in the data source, click the **Mail Merge** button on the Mail Merge toolbar. This will bring up the Merge dialog box, in which a range of records to include in the merge may be specified.

Figure 6-6 Editing a merged document

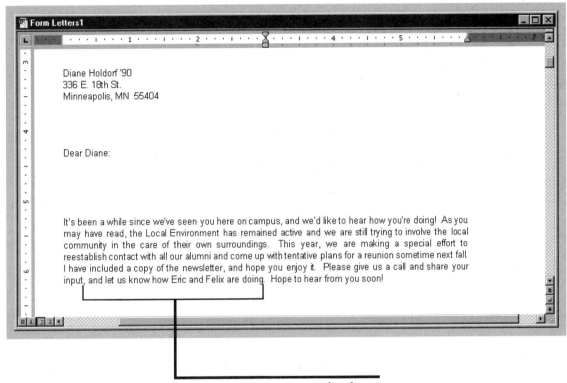

Personalized text

Practice

To practice editing individual merged documents, open the student file **Prac6-5**.

Hot Tip

You can see how the merge fields will look when they are replaced with the specified data by clicking the **View Merged Data** button on the Mail Merge toolbar.

 # Printing Merged Documents

Concept

A merged document can be previewed and printed just like any other Word document.

Do It!

Juan would like to preview his document, then print it and save it.

1 Click the **Print Preview** button on the Standard toolbar. The Print Preview screen appears with six pages showing, as seen in Figure 6-7. (If six pages are not showing, click the **Multiple Pages** button on the Print Preview toolbar and drag all the way down and to the right to select all pages.) Juan notices that the sixth page is blank, and he wants to delete it before printing the document.

2 Click on **page 5** (the one in the upper right corner) to select it. A thin blue border will appear around the page, indicating its selection.

3 Click again on **page 5** to magnify it. The page fills the screen.

4 Click the **Magnifier** button on the Print Preview toolbar to deselect the magnification tool. The mouse pointer will become an I-beam when it is over the page so that the page can be edited.

5 Scroll down the page and place the insertion point in the very last line, which is blank.

6 Press [**Delete**]. The extra blank line disappears and the blank page is deleted with it, leaving the insertion point at the end of the fifth page.

7 Click the **Print** button on the Print Preview toolbar after making sure that your computer is properly connected to a working printer.

8 Click Close on the Print Preview toolbar to get out of Print Preview mode.

9 Click the **Save** button on the Standard toolbar. The Save As dialog box appears.

10 Save the document on your student disk as **MergeDoc**.

More

Using the Print Preview screen makes it possible to quickly spot unwanted variations between different copies of the merged document or to find at a glance problems such as blank pages. If you merged to a new document as in the example above, you may not want to save the newly merged document. If many records were merged or the main document contains graphics and the final merged document is exceedingly long, it may be a better idea to discard the final merged document and save only the main document and the data source. If you need to print it again or modify it later, it only takes the click of a button to merge the document again.

Figure 6-7 Previewing a merged document

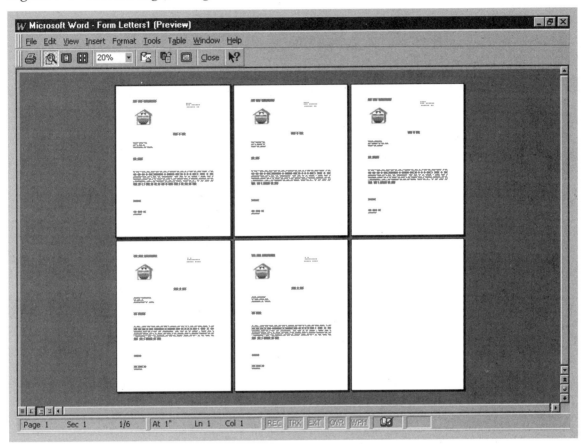

Practice

To practice previewing, printing, and saving a merged document, open the student file **Prac6-6**.

Hot Tip

When previewing merged documents, be especially on the lookout for extra lines being added or removed from subsequent pages; spotting these problems before you print will save a lot of time and paper.

Creating Other Types of Merged Documents

Concept

Word's Mail Merge function can create a variety of document types other than a standard letter or invoice. For example, to mail the form letter that was created in the previous Skill, envelopes could be created with the same data source for each of the five recipients.

Do It!

Juan wants to create **mailing labels** with the same data source used to create the form letter.

1 Click **Tools**, then click **Mail Merge** to bring up the Mail Merge Helper dialog box.

2 Click [Create ▾], then click **Mailing Labels**. A dialog box appears asking whether you want to use the active document window or a new document window.

3 Click [New Main Document]. The dialog box disappears and the document's temporary name is displayed in the Main Document section of the Mail Merge Helper dialog box.

4 Click [Get Data ▾], then click **Open Data Source**. The Open Data Source dialog box appears. You will be using the same data source used to merge the form letter.

5 Select Doit6-4 and click [Open]. A Microsoft Word dialog box appears saying that Word needs to set up the main document.

6 Click [Set Up Main Document]. The **Label Options** dialog box appears, as shown in Figure 6-8. Mailing labels come in sheets ready to print; in this dialog box you must specify what type of labels you will be using.

7 Scroll down through the **Product Number** box and select **5262-Address**.

8 Click [OK]. The **Create Labels** dialog box opens, allowing you to insert merge fields just as you did in the form letter.

9 Click [Insert Merge Field ▾], then click **FirstName**. The field appears on the page.

10 Press **[Space]**.

11 Insert the rest of the fields and characters as follows: **LastName** [Enter] **Address1** [Enter] **City** [,] [Space] **State** [Space] [Space] **Postal Code**. (See Figure 6-9.)

12 Click [OK] to accept the inserted merge fields and return to the Mail Merge Helper dialog box.

More

There are many label formats to choose from, and you may customize the formats to fit any label type that your printer can accommodate. Word can also create main documents in the formats of various envelope shapes and sizes or in catalog format, which essentially lists the records one after the other, each formatted according to the placement of its merge fields. Catalog formatting is useful for parts lists, membership directories, and other such data compilations.

Figure 6-8 Label Options dialog box

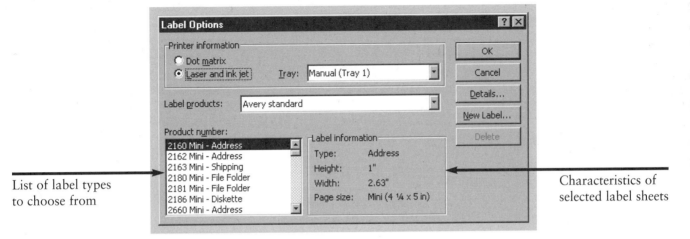

List of label types
to choose from

Characteristics of
selected label sheets

Figure 6-9 Proper placement of Juan's merge fields

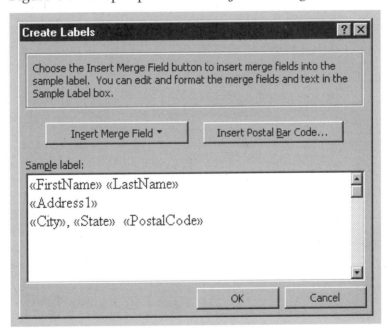

Practice

There is no practice file for this Skill, as an
additional Word file cannot be opened with
the Mail Merge Helper dialog box open.

Hot Tip

If you are creating labels or envelopes to be
mailed within the United States, Word can
automatically print onto the label or envelope a delivery point of address bar code
based on the ZIP code of each record.

Merging and Formatting Labels

Concept

Merged documents can be **formatted** after they have been merged to change their appearance when printed.

Do It!

Juan wants to merge the labels and increase the text size on the finished labels to make them easier to read. Then he will print them and save the file.

1 Click [Merge...] on the Mail Merge Helper dialog box. The Merge dialog box appears, as shown in Figure 6-10.

2 Click [Merge]. The document will merge and should look like Figure 6-11.

3 Press [Ctrl]+[A] to select the entire document.

4 Click the **Font Size** list arrow [ ] on the Formatting toolbar, then click 16. The text on the labels expands. Now they will be more legible when printed.

5 Click the **Print** button [ ] on the Standard toolbar after making sure that your computer is properly connected to a working printer. The merged labels print on plain paper, formatted as they would appear if they were printed on Avery 5262 Address label sheets.

6 Close the document, saving it to your student disk as **Merged Labels**. The unmerged label document reappears in the active window.

7 Close the document, saving it to your student disk as **Unmerged Labels**.

More

To view the formatting changes you have made to a merged label document, you can use the Print Preview command as you did for the form letter. This makes it easier to spot formatting errors, such as a name that spreads to two lines due to its length and an increased font size. As with the form letter, individual records in the final merged document may be edited to fix any individual problems.

Figure 6-10 Merge dialog box

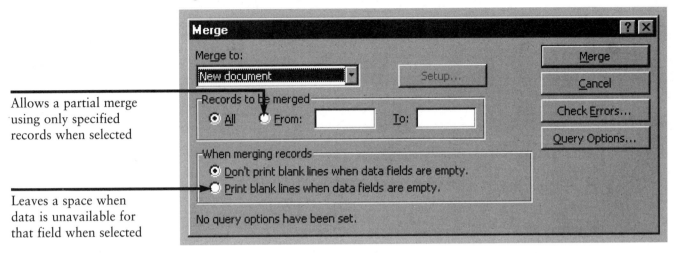

Allows a partial merge
using only specified
records when selected

Leaves a space when
data is unavailable for
that field when selected

Figure 6-11 Merged labels document

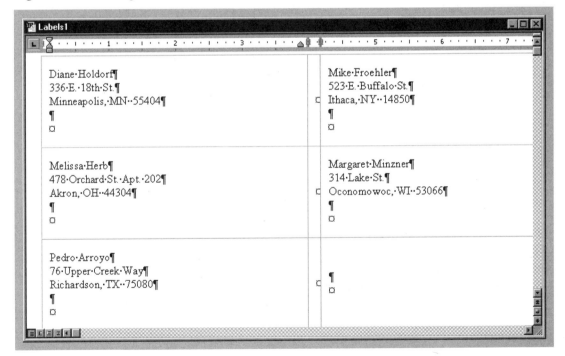

Practice

To practice merging and formatting labels,
open the student file **Prac6-8**.

Hot Tip

If the information in your data source cannot be made to fit a given label, it may be
wise to choose from the product numbers
list an alternate label type that will better
suit your needs.

Shortcuts

Function	Button/Mouse	Menu	Keyboard
Display the Mail Merge Helper dialog box		Click Tools, then click Mail Merge	
Edit a data source			[Alt]+[Shift]+[E]
Insert a field	Insert Merge Field ▾		[Alt]+[Shift]+[F]
Merge documents to a new document			[Alt]+[Shift]+[N]
Merge documents to the printer			[Alt]+[Shift]+[M]
Check for merge errors			

Identify Key Features

Figure 6-12 Identifying the components of the Mail Merge toolbar

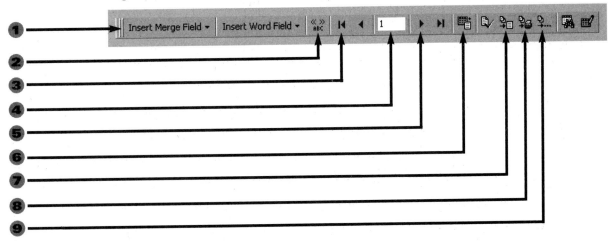

Select the Best Answer

10. Text that is the same for each version of a merged document

11. The place in a main document where data is inserted when the document is merged

12. A command that creates one long document consisting of all versions of a merged document

13. The document containing the individual information for all recipients or items

14. The data pertaining to a single recipient

15. A command that prints merged documents without first creating a document containing all versions

a. Merge field

b. Data source

c. Boilerplate text

d. Merge to New Document

e. Merge to Printer

f. Data record

Quiz (continued)

Complete the Statement

16. To move to the next field in the Data Form dialog box:

    a. Press [Enter]

    b. Press the right arrow key

    c. Press [Tab]

    d. Press [Ctrl]+[Q]

17. When the last field in the current record has been filled, you can open the next blank record by pressing:

    a. [Enter]

    b. The right arrow key

    c. [Tab]

    d. [Ctrl]+[Alt]+[R]

18. The Mail Merge command that allows you to personalize a document is:

    a. Merge to Printer

    b. Edit Data Source

    c. Merge to New Document

    d. Find Record

19. To merge only specified records with the main document, use the:

    a. Merge to Printer command

    b. Mail Merge command

    c. Merge to New Document command

    d. Edit Data Source command

Interactivity

Test Your Skills

1. Create a business letter and turn it into a main document.

   a. Use the Letter Wizard to create a letter to be sent to a mailing list.

   b. Click create, then Form letters.

   c. Click Edit, then the form letter to edit it.

   d. Replace the body text with "The product you ordered is currently on backorder and will be available in 4-6 weeks. Thank you for your patience."

2. Open a data source and insert merge fields into your letter:

   a. From the Mail Merge Helper dialog box, click Get Data and select the student file **Doit6-4**. This is the same data source you used for Juan's form letter.

   b. From the Mail Merge Helper dialog box, click Edit main Document.

   c. Insert merge fields into the letter in the appropriate places.

3. Merge the documents and examine the results on the Print Preview screen:

   a. Click the Merge to New Document button on the Mail Merge toolbar.

   b. Open the Print Preview screen to view the merged documents.

   c. Close the Print Preview screen and all open Word documents. Save the final merged document to your student disk as **Test 6**.

Problem Solving

Using the skills you learned in Lesson 6, open the student file **Problem Solving 6** and save it as **Solved 6**. Open the Mail Merge Helper and create a main document from the active window. Create a data source with at least three records for people you want to send the letter to, with the following fields: FirstName, LastName, Title (Ms./Mr./Mrs.), Address1, Address2, City, State, PostalCode, AmountDue, and PurchaseDate. Insert the merge fields into the main document, replacing the yellow-highlighted placeholders. Near the bottom, insert your name where indicated. After you have inserted the merge fields, add another record to the data source. Then merge the documents to a new document and preview the result. From the Print Preview screen, add a personal note to one of the letters. Finally, print the merged document.

Glossary

A

Alignment

The horizontal position of text within a line or between tab stops. Word's alignment options are right, left, centered, and justified.

Application

See *Program*.

Arrow keys

The [←], [→], [↑], and [↓] keys on the keyboard. Used to move the insertion point, select from a menu or a list of options, or in combination with other keys to execute specific commands.

AutoCorrect

A feature that automatically corrects misspelled words as they are entered. Word provides several entries for commonly misspelled words, but you may also add your own.

AutoFormat

A feature that improves the appearance of a document by applying consistent formatting and styles based on a default document templates or a document template that you specify. The AutoFormat feature can also add bullets or numbers to lists and symbols for trademarks and copyrights where necessary.

Automatic save

A feature that automatically saves document changes in a temporary file at specified intervals. If power to the computer is interrupted, the changes in effect from the last save are retained. Enabled by default, you can turn off this feature from the Save tab of the Options dialog box on the Tools menu.

AutoText entry

A stored text or graphic you want to use again. Global AutoText entries are available to all documents, and may be easily inserted from the AutoText toolbar.

B

Boilerplate text

The text in a mail merge document that is common to all copies of the merged document.

Border

A straight vertical or horizontal line between columns in a section, next to or around paragraphs and graphics, or in a table. You can assign a variety of widths and styles to a border.

Browser

An application that allows you to find and view information on the World Wide Web. Major browsers include Netscape Navigator and Microsoft Internet Explorer.

Bullet

A small graphic, usually a round or square dot, that is commonly used to designate items in a list.

C

Case

Refers to whether or not a letter is capitalized. Some search features are case-sensitive; that is, they will differentiate between words that are spelled the same but have different capitalization.

Cell

The basic unit of a table, separated by gridlines. In a table, the intersection of a row and a column forms one cell.

Cell reference

A code that identifies a cell's position in a table. Each cell reference contains a letter indicating its column and a number indicating its row.

Character style

A combination of character formats from the Font dialog box that is identified by a style name. Changing an element (such as the font size) of a character style changes all text that has been formatted with that style.

Chart

A graphical representation of data.

Click

To press and release a mouse button in one motion; usually refers to the left mouse button.

Clip art

A precreated, usually copyright-free, graphic image that can be inserted into a document to illustrate a point or to add visual interest. Clip art often comes in large collections.

Clip Gallery

A Microsoft Office facility that acts as a library of clip art, pictures, sounds and videos. It allows you to import, store, and reuse these objects in Word documents and in other Office applications.

Clipboard

A temporary storage area for cut or copied text or graphics. You can paste the contents of the Clipboard into any Word document or into a file of another Microsoft Windows program, such as Microsoft PowerPoint. The Clipboard holds the information until it is replaced with another piece of text or a graphic, or until the computer is shut down.

Crop

To hide portions of a graphic that you do not want to appear by resizing its frame. Parts of a graphic that have been cropped can be uncovered later.

Custom dictionary

A document containing all the words that have been "learned" by Word's spell checker. More that one custom dictionary can be created and referenced by a single copy of Microsoft Word.

Cut

To remove selected text or a graphic from a document to the Clipboard so that it may be reinserted elsewhere in the document or in another document.

D

Data source

A table-like document that contains the variable information used with the mail merge feature.

Defaults

Predefined settings for variable items such as page margins, tab spacing, and shortcut key assignments; these can be changed when necessary.

Dialog box

A box that displays the available command options for you to review or change.

Document window

The window on the screen in which a document is viewed and edited. When the document window is maximized, it shares its borders and title bar with the Word application window.

Drag

To hold down the mouse button while moving the mouse.

Drive

The mechanism in a computer that reads recordable media (such as a disk or tape cartridge) to retrieve and store information. Personal computers often have one hard disk drive labeled C, a drive that reads floppy disks labeled A, and a drive that reads cds labeled D.

Drop cap

A formatting option in which the first letter of a paragraph expands greatly in size; usually used at the beginning of a chapter or other major section of a document.

E

Edit

To add, delete, or modify text or other elements of a file.

Effects

Text formats such as small caps, all caps, hidden text, strikethrough, subscript, or superscript.

Extend selection

To increase the selected area. When a selection is extended, it grows progressively larger each time [F8] is pressed. To shrink the selection, press [Shift]+[F8]. The arrow keys, or any of the other keys that move the insertion point within text, may also be used to enlarge or shrink the selection.

F

Field

The place in a main document where a specific portion of a record, such a a postal code, will be inserted when the document is merged. Also known as a merge field.

File

A document that has been created and saved under a unique file name. In Word, all documents and pictures are stored as files.

Folders

Subdivisions of a disk that work like a filing system to help you organize files.

Font

A name given to a collection of text characters at a certain size, weight, and style. Font has become synonymous with typeface. Arial and Times New Roman are examples of font names.

Font size
Refers to the physical size of text, measured in points (pts). The more points, the larger the appearance of the text on the page.

Font style
Refers to whether text appears as bold, italicized, or underlined, or any combination of these formats.

Format
The way text appears on a page. In Word formats comes from direct formatting or the application of styles. The four formatting levels are character, paragraph, section, and document.

Frame
A box that appears around an inserted object (such as a graphic) in a document so that it may be easily resized or positioned on a page.

G

Global template
In Word, a template named NORMAL.DOT that contains default menus, autocorrect entries, styles and page setup settings. Documents use the global template unless a custom template is specified. See also *template*.

Graphic
A picture, chart, or drawing in a document.

Graphic object
An element in a document that can be moved, sized, and modified without leaving Word.

Gridlines
The lines that separate cells in a table. Gridlines do not print. You can alternately hide and display gridlines with the Gridlines command on the Table menu.

H

Hanging indent
A paragraph format in which the first line of a paragraph extends farther to the left than subsequent lines.

Header and footer
A header is an item or group of items that appears at the top of every page in a section. A footer appears at the bottom of every page. Headers and footers often contain page numbers, chapter titles, dates, and author names.

Hidden text
A character format that allows you to show or hide designated text. Word indicates hidden text by underlining it with a dotted line. You can select or clear the Hidden Text option with the Options command on the Tools menu. Hidden text may be omitted when printing.

Horizontal ruler
A bar displayed across the top of the document window in all views. The ruler can be used to indent paragraphs, set tab stops, adjust left and right paragraph margins, and change column widths in a table. You can hide this ruler by clicking View, then clicking Ruler.

HTML
An acronym for HyperText Markup Language, which is the language that defines the way information is presented on a Web page. Word can automatically convert the formatting you have given a document into HTML, which functionally turns your document into a Web page.

HTTP
An acronym for HyperText Transfer Protocol; appears at the beginning of a URL to notify the browser that the following information is a hypertext Web document.

Hyperlink
Originated as an element of Web page design; usually text, clicking a hyperlink brings you directly to a predefined location within a document or to a specific page on the World Wide Web.

I

Indent
The distance between text boundaries and page margins. Positive indents make the text area narrower than the space between margins. Negative indents allow text to extend into the margins. A paragraph can have left, right, and first-line indents.

Insertion point
A vertical blinking line on the Word screen that indicates where text and graphics will be inserted. The insertion point also determines where Word will begin an action.

L

Landscape
A term used to refer to horizontal page orientation; opposite of "portrait," or vertical, orientation.

Line break
A mark inserted where you want to end one line and start another without starting a new paragraph. A line break may be inserted by pressing [Shift]+[Return].

Line spacing
The height of a line of text, often measured in lines or points.

M

Mail merge
The creation of personalized form letters or labels by combining boilerplate text with variable information.

Main document
In the mail merge process the main document is the document that contains the text that is the same in each version of the merged document.

Margin
The distance between the edge of the text in the document and the top, bottom, or side edges of the page.

Maximize
To enlarge a window to its maximum size. Maximizing an application window causes it to fill the screen; maximizing a document window causes it to fill the application window.

Menu bar
Lists the names of menus containing Word commands. Click a menu name on the menu bar to display a list of commands.

Minimize
To shrink a window to its minimum size. Minimizing an application window reduces it to a button on the Windows taskbar; minimizing a document window reduces it to a short title bar in the application window.

N

Non-printing characters
Marks displayed on the screen to indicate characters that do not print, such as paragraph marks or dots indicating spaces. You can control the display of these characters with the Options command on the Tools menu, and the Show/Hide ¶ button on the Standard toolbar.

Normal view
The view you see when you start Word. Normal view is used for most editing and formatting tasks. Normal view shows text formatting but simplifies the layout of the page so that you can type and edit quickly. If a document is displayed in another view, you can switch to normal view by clicking Normal on the View menu.

Note pane
A special window in which the text of all the footnotes in a document appears. The note pane can be accessed by double-clicking a note reference mark.

O

Object
A table, chart, graphic, equation, or other form of information you create and edit with a program other than Word, but whose data you insert and store in a Word document.

Office Assistant
An animated manifestation of the Microsoft Office 97 help facility. The Office Assistant provides hints, instructions, and a convenient interface between the user and Word's various help features.

Options
The choices available in a dialog box.

Overtype
An option for replacing existing characters one by one as you type. You can select overtype by selecting the Overtype option on the Edit tab with the Options command on the Tools menu. When you select the Overtype option, the letters "OVR" appear in the status bar at the bottom of the Word window. You can also double-click these letters in the status bar to activate or deactivate overtype mode.

P

Page break
The point at which one page ends and another begins. A break you insert is called a hard break; a break determined by the page layout is called a soft break. In Normal View, a hard break appears as a dotted line and is labeled Page Break, while a soft break appears as a dotted line without a label.

Page Layout View
A view of a document as it will appear when you print it. Items such as headers, footnotes, and framed objects appear in their actual positions, and you can drag them to new positions.

Paragraph style
A stored set of paragraph format settings.

Paste
To insert cut or copied text into a document from the Clipboard.

Path
The address of a file's location. It contains the drive, folder and subfolders, and file name. For example, the complete path for Microsoft Word might be C:\Program Files\Microsoft Office\Office\Winword.exe.

Point size
A measurement used for the size of text characters. There are 72 points per inch.

Portrait
A term used to refer to vertical page orientation; opposite of "landscape," or horizontal, orientation.

Position
The specific placement of graphics, tables, and paragraphs on a page. In Word, you can assign items to fixed positions on a page.

Program
A software application that performs specific tasks, such as Microsoft Word or Microsoft Excel.

Program window
A window that contains the running program. The window displays the menus and provides the workspace for any document used within the application. The application window shares its borders and title bar with maximized document windows.

R

Record
The entire collection of fields related to a particular item or individual, contained in the data source.

Redo
Counteracts the Undo command by repeating previously reversed actions or changes, usually editing or formatting commands. Only actions that have been undone can be reversed with the redo command.

Resize
To change the size of an object (such as framed text or a graphic) by dragging sizing handles located on the sides and corner of the selected object, or by adjusting its dimensions in a dialog box.

Right-click
To click the right mouse button; often necessary to access specialized menus and shortcuts. (The designated right and left mouse buttons may be reversed with the Mouse control panel to accomodate user preferences.)

S

Sans serif font
A font whose characters do not include serifs, the small strokes at the ends of the characters. Arial and Helvetica are sans serif fonts.

ScreenTip
A brief explanation of a button or object that appears when the mouse pointer is paused over it. Other ScreenTips are accessed by clicking What's This from the Help menu and then clicking a particular item, or by clicking the question mark button in the title bar of dialog boxes.

Scroll bar
A graphical device for moving vertically and horizontally through a document with the mouse. Scroll bars are located alomg the right and bottom edges of the document window.

Section
A part of a document separated from the rest of the document by a section break. By separating a document into sections, you can use different page and column formatting in different parts of the same document.

Selection bar
An invisible column at the left edge of a column of text used to select text with the mouse. In a table, each cell has its own selection bar at the left edge of the cell.

Serif font
A font that has small strokes at the ends of the characters. Times New Roman and Palatino are serif fonts.

Shading
The background color or pattern behind text or graphics.

Soft return
A line break created by pressing [Shift]+[Enter]. This creates a new line without creating a new paragraph.

Spreadsheet program
A software program used for calculations and financial analysis.

Standard toolbar

A row of buttons that perform some of the most frequently used commands, such as Open, Print and Save. Usually located under the menu bar.

Status bar

Located at the bottom of the Word window, it displays the current page number and section number, the total number of pages in the document, and the vertical position of the insertion point. It also indicates whether certain options are active.

Style

A group of formatting instructions that you name and store, and are able to modify. When you apply a style to selected characters and paragraphs, all the formatting instructions of that style are applied at once.

Style Gallery

A feature that allows you to examine the overall formatting and styles used in a document template. With the Style Gallery you can also preview your document formatted in the styles from a selected template.

T

Tab stop

A measured position for placing and aligning text at a specific distance along a line. Word has four kinds of tab stops, left-aligned (the default), centered, right-aligned, and decimal. Tab stops are shown on the horizontal ruler.

Table

One or more rows of cells commonly used to display numbers and other data for quick reference and analysis. Items in a table are organized into rows and columns. You can convert text into a table with the Insert Table command on the Table menu.

Template

A special kind of document that provides basic tools and text for creating a document. Templates can contain styles, AutoText items, macros, customized menu and key assignments, and text or graphics that are the same in different types of document.

Text box

A rectangular area in which text is added so that it may be manipulated independently of the rest of a document. Text boxes may be rotated or flipped, formatted with 3-D effects or shadows, or linked together so that text flows between them.

Text wrap

Automatic placement of a word on the next line when there is not enough room for it on the current line.

Title bar

The horizontal bar at the top of a window that displays the name of the document or application that appears in that window.

Toolbar

A graphical bar containing several buttons that act as shortcuts for many common Word commands.

U

Undo

A command that lets you reverse previous actions or changes, usually editing or formatting actions. Actions from the File menu cannot be reversed. You can undo up to 100 previous actions from the time you opened the document.

URL

An acronym for Uniform Resource Locator; an address specifying where a particular piece of information can be found. A Web address is a kind of URL.

V

Vertical alignment

The placement of text on a page in relation to the top, bottom, or center of the page.

Vertical ruler

A graphical bar displayed at the left edge of the document window in the page layout and print preview views. You can use this ruler to adjust the top and bottom page margins, and change row height in a table.

View

A display that shows certain aspects of the document. Word has seven views: normal, online layout, page layout, outline, master document, full screen, and print preview.

View buttons

Appear in the horizontal scroll bar. Allow you to display the document in one of three views: Normal, Page Layout and Outline.

W

Window

A rectangular area on the screen in which you view and work on documents.

Wizard

A helpful program you use to create documents. When you use a wizard to create a document, you are asked a series of questions about document preferences, and then the wizard creates the document to meet your specifications.

Word processing program

Software used to create documents efficiently. Usually includes features beyond simple editing, such as formatting and arranging text and graphics to create attractive documents.

World Wide Web

A major component of the Internet, which is a vast global network of smaller networks and personal computers. Web pages include hyperlinks and present information in a graphical format that can incorporate text, graphics, sounds, and digital movies.

WYSIWYG

An acronym for What You See Is What You Get; indicates that a document will print out with the same formatting that is displayed in the document window.

Index